THE GRANNY SQUARE BOOK

Creative Publishing international

Copyright © 2011 Creative Publishing international, Inc.

First published in the United States of America by
Creative Publishing international, Inc., a member of
Quayside Publishing Group
400 First Avenue North
Suite 300
Minneapolis, MN 55401
1-800-328-3895
www.creativepub.com

ISBN-13: 978-1-58923-638-7

10 9 8 7 6 5 4 3 2 1

Library of Congress Cataloging-in-Publication Data
Hubert, Margaret.
 The granny square book : timeless techniques and fresh ideas for crocheting square by square / Margaret Hubert.
  p. cm.
 Summary: """Techniques for crocheting granny squares with basic instructions, 75 stitch patterns, and a variety of projects"--Provided by publisher"-- Provided by publisher.
 ISBN-13: 978-1-58923-638-7 (spiral bound)
 ISBN-10: 1-58923-638-6 (hard cover)
 1. Crocheting--Patterns. I. Title.

TT820.H8326 2011
746.43'4--dc23

                            2011013365

Technical Editor: Karen Manthey
Copy Editor: India Tresselt
Proofreader: Karen Ruth
Cover Design: Mighty Media
Book Design & Page Layout: Cindy LaBreacht
Stitch diagrams: Karen Manthey
Photographs, pg 6, 7, 8, 140 and 142: Christopher Hubert

Printed in China

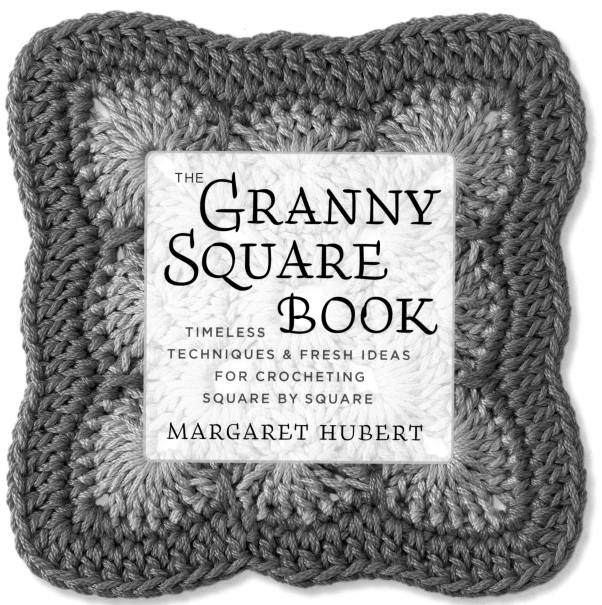

THE GRANNY SQUARE BOOK

TIMELESS
TECHNIQUES & FRESH IDEAS
FOR CROCHETING
SQUARE BY SQUARE

MARGARET HUBERT

ACKNOWLEDGMENTS

It takes a group of very talented people to get a book from "I have an idea" to seeing it in print. Some of these wonderful people are listed below, but my thanks also go out to all the people behind the scenes, who work so hard in the many departments of publishing.

Linda Neubauer, my editor. If not for Linda, there would be no book. Linda has always believed in me, is always there for me, and always helps when some technical aspects are beyond my capability.

Karen Manthey, technical editor and diagram illustrator, who always creates easy-to-follow, wonderful diagrams.

Tahki/Stacy Charles Yarns. Diane Friedman and Stacy Charles have so generously donated the yarn for all the swatches in the book and for four of the projects. They are great supporters of crochet and are always willing to help designers.

Other yarn companies that I would like to thank, who have gladly donated yarn, and without whose support designers could not work: Blue Heron Yarns (blueheronyarns.com), Kreinik (kreinik.com), Caron (naturallycaron.com), Lion Brand (lionbrand.com), Patons (patonsyarns.com), Plymouth Yarn (plymouthyarn.com), Premier Yarns (premieryarns.com), Red Heart Yarns (redheartyarns.com), have all donated yarns for the special projects in the book.

Jeannine Buehler, Paula Alexander, Nancy Smith, and Jennifer Radinsky, who helped me to crochet all the projects in the book.

Elaine Brown, who designed and made the hat topper.

Chris Simon, who allowed me to use her wonderful Butterfly Square, used for the Butterfly Garden Two-Way Shawl.

Sharon Valencia, my daughter, who designed and made the Yoga Tunic and Mat Carrier.

Nicole Valencia, my granddaughter, who designed (and made with her mom's help) the Bright Colors Backpack and the Tween Hooded Vest.

Chris Hubert, my son, who took several of the family photographs and also the photographs of the older afghans.

Many thanks to all.

Dedication

I would like to dedicate this book to all of my wonderful family for their support, especially my daughter Sharon, my granddaughter Nicole, and my son Chris, who gave a little more of themselves for this book.

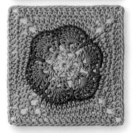

Contents

INTRODUCTION

Many who know me as a crochet and knitwear designer may think that my doing a book on granny squares is a little odd. After all, isn't the granny square a bit dated and boringly basic? Far from it! The granny square is the foundation upon which unlimited new and exciting designs can be created.

Mom and I collaborated on this afghan fifty years ago and it is still keeping someone warm today.

The term granny square really encompasses scores of unique motifs, and I've included seventy-five of them in this book. With the marvelous selection of yarns available to us today, you need only some basic design instruction and a little imagination to take any of these motifs to new creative heights. It's amazing what you can do with the humble granny square.

My love affair with the granny began in 1954 when I learned to crochet. I had been knitting for years, having learned at a very young age and loving it, but crocheting was a new and exciting adventure for me. Picking up border stitches on the front of a knitted sweater to crochet a simple border was my first step into the world of crochet. Next was learning to make a granny square. My mother was a fabulous knitter, did not crochet very much and never taught me how, but when she saw me making these captivating little squares over and over again, she was hooked. Together we made a huge granny afghan, Mom making all the little squares, me doing the edging and putting it together. After using it for many years, I passed it along to a dear friend, Carol, who still loves and cares for it.

In 1975, I decided to make myself a granny square bedspread using cotton thread. It was a project that spanned six years. It was initially made to fit a standard size bed; a few years later I added rows to fit a queen size and later added more squares and rows to fit a king size bed. I still love it and use it.

The tradition of the granny square is passed down from one generation to the next. Each generation leaves its own design imprint on granny square history, influenced by important events of their era, the current styles, and the yarns available to them. I taught my daughter to make her first granny square when she was seven. She made a giant granny square and presented me with her first afghan. Sharon had two granny square designs published when she was just a teenager.

After all this work, I could never bear to part with it!

My daughter is still proud of the first granny square afghan she ever made.

My daughter and I both taught my granddaughter to crochet, and she is already designing her own projects with grannies. With her mother's help, she designed and crocheted the adorable backpack taught on page 140.

Working on this book led me to wonder how many of my fellow designers learned to crochet at an early age and if they learned from a grandparent or parent. I was particularly interested in knowing if they learned to make granny squares at a young age, and if they were passing on their knowledge to others, so I asked a number of friends, who happen also to be fabulous crochet designers, about their early experiences. Here are some of the replies that I received; very interesting and varied:

I learned to crochet from my mother when I was nine years old in 1973. The granny square was probably the second thing that she taught me how to crochet. (The first was single crochet in rows and it bored me.)
—VASHTI BRAHA

My second grade teacher offered to stay after school and teach crochet to any students who wished to learn. I was the only one who stayed! Years later I tracked her down to thank her, and she now works from some of my patterns.
—TAMMY HILDEBRAND

(continued)

Designed by my granddaughter, this backpack shows her favorite colors and her love of anything denim.

INTRODUCTION (continued)

My mum had taught me to knit when I was quite small, but I don't remember her crocheting very much. I just sort of figured it out for myself when I was in my teens, when crochet hippy-style fashions were starting to come into vogue. I never actually made a granny square back then although soon after I started crocheting I remember I did create a very bright and lacy "granny circle" poncho using random circular motifs simply because I hadn't yet figured out how to put in the corners!

—PRUDENCE MAPSTONE

I didn't learn to crochet until age twenty-two when I was a Peace Corps volunteer in Honduras. I learned by rote in Spanish. I have passed on the skills to both of my daughters, and one crochets more than the other.

—GWEN BLAKLEY KINSLER

I learned how to crochet from my mother when I was in the sixth grade because I saw her making granny squares and was dying to learn how to make them too. Since my mother is left-handed and I am not, it turns out that I was crocheting "wrong" like she did for thirty years before someone pointed it out! My teen-aged daughter is a sporadic crocheter—her favorite projects are long, skinny scarves and amigurumi.

—MARY BETH TEMPLE

YES! My mom did teach me when I was young. She taught me to sew and crochet, and we made stuff for Barbie! Not many granny squares until 1990 when I picked up a couple afghan books that rekindled my love for crochet. That's when I went granny square nuts. THEN I discovered Freeform and the whole world changed! Recently Mom and I were crocheting together and she was asking me lots of questions. I kept saying, but you taught me!

—MYRA WOOD

Grannies really do span the generations. If you love to crochet, teach someone younger. If you don't have a son or daughter to teach, maybe a relative or friend. A few simple lessons will equip someone for their lifetime journey of crochet learning and enjoyment. Keep the granny square going!

I hope that you enjoy the book as much as I have enjoyed doing it.

Margaret Hubert

CROCHET BASICS

In this section you will find an overview of the basic techniques and tools used for crocheting and for making granny squares. Use this section to refresh your memory on any of the basics if you've become a little rusty. Or if you are new to crochet, this is a good place to begin.

HOOKS AND OTHER NOTIONS

Crochet hooks are available in a range of standard sizes, and they can be made from metal, wood, bamboo, or plastic. Hooks may have slightly different shapes at the neck or hook, but their sizes, designated with letters, numbers, and metric diameter measurements, are universally used. In simple terms, the diameter of the shaft determines the size of the stitch a hook will make. The chart at right shows the correspondence between the letter and number sizes and the metric conversions. In addition to hooks, there are only a few other tools a crocheter needs. The list includes a tape measure, scissors for cutting yarn, stitch markers, and tapestry or yarn needles for sewing seams.

CROCHET HOOK SIZES

Metric Size	U.S. Size
2.25 mm	B/1
2.75 mm	C/2
3.25 mm	D/3
3.5 mm	E/4
3.75 mm	F/5
4 mm	G/6
4.5 mm	7
5 mm	H/8
5.5 mm	I/9
6 mm	J/10
6.5 mm	K/10½
8 mm	L/11
9 mm	M/N/13
10 mm	N/P/15
15 mm	P/Q
16 mm	Q
19 mm	S

NOTE: Steel hooks are sized differently than regular hooks: the higher the number, the smaller the hook. They range from the smallest #14 or .9 mm to the largest of #00 or 2.7 mm.

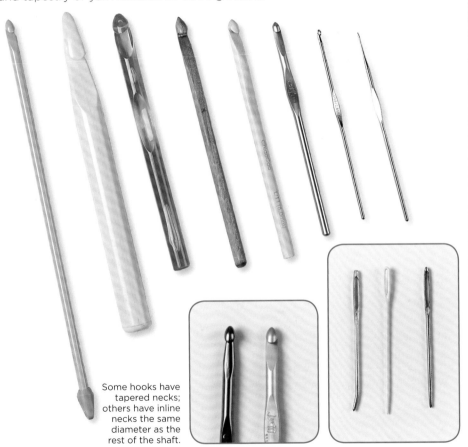

Some hooks have tapered necks; others have inline necks the same diameter as the rest of the shaft.

Yarn needles have a large eye for carrying the yarn and blunt tips to insert through stitches. The bent-tip style is particularly helpful for sewing seams.

GENERAL TECHNIQUES

Granny squares can incorporate any crochet stitch. Along with the following guide to the stitches you may encounter, you will also find information about how crochet directions are written and how to interpret the stitch diagrams.

STITCHES

SLIP KNOT

Make a loop several inches from the end of the yarn, insert the hook through the loop, and catch the tail with the end (1). Draw the yarn through the loop on the hook (2). Pull on the tail to tighten the slip knot around the hook.

CHAIN

After the slip knot, start your chain. Wrap the yarn over the hook (yarn over) and catch it with the hook. Draw the yarn through the loop on the hook. You have now made one chain. Repeat the process to make a row of chains. When counting chains, do not count the slip knot at the beginning or the loop that is on the hook.

SLIP STITCH

The slip stitch is a very short stitch, which is mainly used to join two pieces of crochet together when working in rounds. To make a slip stitch, insert the hook into the specified stitch, wrap the yarn over the hook, and then draw the yarn through the stitch and the loop already on the hook.

SINGLE CROCHET

Insert the hook into the specified stitch, wrap the yarn over the hook, and draw the yarn through the stitch so there are two loops on the hook (1). Wrap the yarn over the hook again and draw the yarn through both loops (2). When working in single crochet, always insert the hook through both top loops of the next stitch, unless the directions specify front loop or back loop only.

HALF DOUBLE CROCHET

Wrap the yarn over the hook, insert the hook into the specified stitch, and wrap the yarn over the hook again. Draw the yarn through the stitch so there are three loops on the hook (1). Wrap the yarn over the hook and draw it through all three loops at once (2).

DOUBLE CROCHET

Wrap the yarn over the hook, insert the hook into the specified stitch, and wrap the yarn over the hook again. Draw the yarn through the stitch so there are three loops on the hook (1). Wrap the yarn over the hook again and draw it

through two of the loops so there are now two loops on the hook (2). Wrap the yarn over the hook again and draw it through the last two loops (3).

TRIPLE CROCHET

Wrap the yarn over the hook twice, insert the hook into the specified stitch, and wrap the yarn over the hook again. Draw the yarn through the stitch so there are four loops on the hook. Wrap the yarn over the hook again (1) and draw it through two of the loops so there are now three loops on the hook (2). Wrap the yarn over the hook again and draw it through two of the loops so there are now two loops on the hook (3). Wrap the yarn over the hook again and draw it through the last two loops (4).

DOUBLE TRIPLE CROCHET

Wrap the yarn over the hook three times, insert the hook into the specified stitch, and wrap the yarn over the hook again. Draw the yarn through the stitch so there are five loops on the hook. Wrap the yarn over the hook again and draw it through two of the loops so there are now four loops on the hook. Wrap the yarn over the hook again and draw it through two of the loops so there are now three loops on the hook. Wrap the yarn over the hook again and draw it through two of the loops so there are now two loops on the hook. Wrap the yarn over the hook again and draw it through the last two loops.

WORKING THROUGH THE BACK LOOP

This creates a distinct ridge on the side facing you. Insert the hook through the back loop only of each stitch, rather than under both loops of the stitch. Complete the stitch as usual.

SINGLE CROCHET TWO STITCHES TOGETHER

This decreases the number of stitches in a row or round by one. Insert the hook into the specified stitch, wrap the yarn over the hook, and draw the yarn through the stitch so there are two loops on the hook. Insert the hook through the next stitch, wrap the yarn over the hook, and draw the yarn through the stitch so there are three loops on the hook (1). Wrap the yarn over the hook again and draw the yarn through all the loops at once (2).

DOUBLE CROCHET TWO STITCHES TOGETHER

This decreases the number of stitches in a row or round by one. Wrap the yarn over the hook, insert the hook into the specified stitch, and wrap the yarn over the hook again. Draw the yarn through the stitch so there are three loops on the hook. Wrap the yarn over the hook again and draw it through two of the loops so there are now two loops on the hook. Wrap the yarn over the hook and pick up a loop in the next stitch, so there are now four loops on the hook. Wrap the yarn over the hook and draw through two loops. Wrap the yarn over and draw through three loops to complete the stitch.

FRONT POST DOUBLE CROCHET

This stitch follows a row of double crochet. Chain 3 to turn. Wrap the yarn over the hook. Working from the front, insert the hook from right to left (left to right for left-handed crocheters) under the post of the first double crochet from the previous row and pick up a loop (shown). Wrap the yarn over the hook and complete the stitch as a double crochet.

REVERSE SINGLE CROCHET

This stitch is usually used to create a border. At the end of a row, chain 1 but do not turn. Working backward, insert the hook into the previous stitch (1), wrap the yarn over the hook, and draw the yarn through the stitch so there are two loops on the hook. Wrap the yarn over the hook again and draw the yarn through both loops. Continue working in the reverse direction (2).

SHELL

There are many types of shell stitches. Here is one example.

Make two double crochets, chain 1, and then work two more double crochets in the same stitch (shown). This is often called a cluster. In the following row, work the same cluster into the space created by the chain stitch. Other versions of the shell stitch may have more than two double crochets and more than one chain stitch between them.

 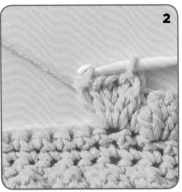

POPCORN

(Worked from the right side.) Make five double crochets in the specified stitch, draw up the last loop slightly, and remove the hook (1). Insert the hook into the first of the five double crochets made, pick up the dropped loop, and draw it through. Chain 1 (2).

BULLION

Chain 3. Wrap the yarn loosely around the hook ten times, insert the hook in the next stitch, yarn over, and draw up a loop (1). Wrap the yarn over the hook again and carefully draw through the coil of loops on the hook. You may find it necessary to pick the loops off the hook with your fingers, one at a time (2). Yarn over the hook again and draw through the remaining stitch.

PICOT

This stitch pattern is used as an edging.

*Chain 3, work one single crochet in the first chain (1), skip one stitch, and work one single crochet in the next stitch. Repeat from * across the row (2).

CROCHET INSTRUCTIONS

Crochet instructions are written in a shortened form, using standard abbreviations (see page 18). Diagrams with symbols that represent the stitches are often given along with the written instructions, or sometimes the diagrams stand alone (see page 19).

READING WRITTEN INSTRUCTIONS

Crochet patterns are often groups of stitches that are repeated a certain number of times in a row or round. The stitch group is enclosed between brackets [ ] or parentheses ( ) immediately followed by the number of times to work the stitches. For example: [ch 1, sk 1, 1 dc in next st] 4 times. Another way to indicate repeated stitch patterns is with asterisks. This same instruction could be written: *ch 1, sk 1, 1 dc in next st, repeat from * 3 times more.

Parentheses are also used to clarify or reinforce information: ch 3 (counts as 1 dc). They may be used at the end of a row to tell you how many total stitches you should have in that row, such as (25 sc). Sometimes this information is set off with a dash at the row end—25 sc. Parentheses are also used to tell you which side of the work you should be on: (WS) or (RS). For multisize patterns, parentheses enclose the variations you must apply to the different sizes. For example, a pattern may include directions for size 2 (4, 6, 8). Throughout the instructions, wherever you must choose for the correct size, the choices will be written like this: ch 34 (36, 38, 40).

TERM CONVERSIONS

Crochet techniques are the same universally, and everyone uses the same terms. However, US patterns and UK patterns are different because the terms denote different stitches. Here is a conversion chart to explain the differences.

US	UK
single crochet (sc)	double crochet (dc)
half double crochet (hdc)	half treble (htr)
double crochet (dc)	treble (tr)
triple crochet (tr)	double treble (dtr)

READING SYMBOLS

Symbol diagrams are another way to convey crochet instructions. Every symbol in the diagram represents a specific stitch as it appears from the right side of the work. For granny squares, the rounds are marked on the diagram, beginning at the center. The diagram is accompanied by a key to help you identify the symbols. Though there may be some subtle differences in the way the symbols look, designers use a standard set of symbols.

ABBREVIATIONS

Here is the list of standard abbreviations used for crochet.

approx	approximately
beg	begin/beginning
bet	between
BL	back loop(s)
bo	bobble
BP	back post
BPdc	back post double crochet
BPsc	back post single crochet
CC	contrasting color
ch	chain
ch-	refers to chain or space previously made, e.g., ch-1 space
ch lp	chain loop
ch-sp	chain space
CL	cluster(s)
cm	centimeter(s)
cont	continue
dc	double crochet
dc2tog	double crochet 2 stitches together
dec	decrease/decreases/decreasing
dtr	double triple
FL	front loop(s)
foll	follow/follows/following
FP	front post

FPdc	front post double crochet
FPsc	front post single crochet
g	gram(s)
hdc	half double crochet
inc	increase/increases/increasing
lp(s)	loop(s)
Lsc	long single crochet
m	meter(s)
MC	main color
mm	millimeter(s)
oz	ounce(s)
p	picot
patt	pattern
pc	popcorn
pm	place marker
prev	previous
rem	remain/remaining
rep	repeat(s)
rev sc	reverse single crochet
rnd(s)	round(s)
RS	right side(s)
sc	single crochet
sc2tog	single crochet 2 stitches together
sk	skip

Sl st	slip stitch
sp(s)	space(s)
st(s)	stitch(es)
tbl	through back loop(s)
tch	turning chain
tfl	through front loop(s)
tog	together
tr	triple crochet
trtr	triple treble crochet
tr2tog	triple crochet 2 stitches together
WS	wrong side(s)
yd	yard(s)
yo	yarn over
[ ]	Work instructions within brackets as many times as directed
( )	Work instructions within prentheses as many times as directed
*	Repeat instructions following the single asterisk as directed
* *	Repeat instructions between asterisks as many times as directed or repeat from a given set of instructions

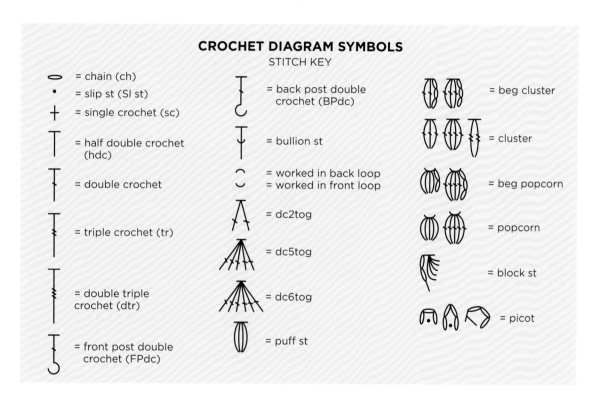

CROCHET DIAGRAM SYMBOLS
STITCH KEY

⬯	= chain (ch)
•	= slip st (Sl st)
+	= single crochet (sc)
	= half double crochet (hdc)
	= double crochet
	= triple crochet (tr)
	= double triple crochet (dtr)
	= front post double crochet (FPdc)
	= back post double crochet (BPdc)
	= bullion st
⌒ ⌣	= worked in back loop / = worked in front loop
	= dc2tog
	= dc5tog
	= dc6tog
	= puff st
	= beg cluster
	= cluster
	= beg popcorn
	= popcorn
	= block st
	= picot

A WORD ABOUT GAUGE

Every pattern will tell you the exact yarn (or weight of yarn) to use, and suggest what size hook to use to crochet an item with the same finished measurements as the project shown. It is important to choose yarn in the weight specified in order to successfully complete the project. The hook size recommended is the size an average crocheter would use to get the correct gauge. Gauge refers to the number of stitches and the number of rows in a given width and length, usually in 4" (10 cm), of crocheted fabric. For this book, gauge also refers to the finished size of a granny square.

Before beginning to crochet a project, it is very important to take the time to check your gauge. Crochet a sample swatch of the stitch pattern or crochet one of the granny squares used in the project. If you have more stitches to the inch or if your square is smaller than the instructions call for, you are working tighter than average; try a new swatch or square with a larger hook. If you have fewer stitches to the inch or if your square is larger than the instructions call for, you are working looser than average; try a smaller hook.

NOTE: Always change hook size to get proper gauge, rather than trying to work tighter or looser.

GRANNY SQUARE TECHNIQUES

Crocheting a project square by square has a lot of perks. Because you are working on small pieces at a time, you can take your project with you and work inconspicuously if necessary. Completion of every square gives you a tiny rush of satisfaction, and watching the squares stack up gives you a strong feeling of accomplishment. The final step of joining the squares is very relaxing and rewarding.

GETTING STARTED

Most granny squares are worked in rounds, beginning with a center ring. There are different ways to begin the ring. The method you choose may depend on whether you want the center to be open or tightly closed.

CHAIN RING

The most usual method of beginning working in rounds is by making a foundation chain, joining with a slip stitch to form a ring (1), then work the next round inserting the hook into the center of the ring rather than in the chain stitches (2). In this method the size of the ring is fixed and cannot be tightened.

SLIP KNOT

1. Form a loose slip knot. Holding the tail between
   your thumb and middle finger, work the first round of stitches into the slip knot.

2. Before joining the round, gently pull the tail of the knot to tighten the center.

ADJUSTABLE LOOP

A third method, sometimes referred to as magic ring or sliding loop also allows you to pull the ring tightly closed.

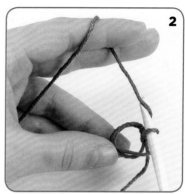

1. Wrap the yarn clockwise around your index finger twice, leaving a 6" (15.2 cm) tail. Holding the tail between your thumb and middle finger, slide the hook under the wraps and catch the working yarn.

2. Pull the working yarn through the ring, and chain the designated number of stitches.

3. Work additional stitches into the two loops of the ring, keeping the tail free. Before joining the round, pull on the tail a little; one loop will tighten slightly. Pull on that loop, which will tighten the other loop.

4. Then pull the tail which will tighten the remaining loop.

How to Crochet a Classic Granny Square

Most granny squares are worked in rounds instead of rows. A classic granny begins with a foundation chain formed in a circle.

1. **FOUNDATION RND:** With A, ch 4, join with a Sl st to form a ring.

2. **RND 1:** With A, ch 3 (counts as a dc), work 2 more dc in ring, *ch 3, work 3 more dc in ring, rep from * twice more, join with a Sl st to 3rd ch of beg ch 3.

(continued)

3. **RND 2:** Join B by making a slip knot on hook, place hook in any corner ch-3 sp, pick up a loop, yo through 2 (1 ch made), ch 2 more for beg chain (A). 2 dc in same ch-3 sp (half corner made), *ch 2 [3 dc, ch 3, 3 dc] in next ch-3 sp (corner made) (B), rep from * twice, ch 2, 3 dc in same sp as beg ch-3, ch 3, join with a Sl st to 3rd ch of beg ch-3 (C).

4. **RND 3:** Join A with a slip knot (same as rnd 2), make 2 more dc in same ch 3 sp (half corner made), *ch 2, 3 dc in next ch-2 sp, ch 2, [3 dc, ch 3, 3 dc] in next ch-3 sp (corner made), rep from * twice, ch 2, 3 dc in next ch-2 sp, ch 2, 3 dc in same sp as beg half corner, ch 3, join with a Sl st to 3rd ch of beg ch-3, fasten off.

If you love multicolored squares but hate all the ends created by changing yarns, you might try one of the great new self-striping yarns such as Bernat Mosaic. Believe it or not, all these Classic Granny Squares (page 32) are made from the same ball, no joining for color changes.

DETAILS AND FINISHING

A WORD ABOUT BEGINNING CHAINS

When you crochet in rows, you alternate from right side to wrong side with each row. At the end of each row, you crochet a turning chain of one to four chains, depending on the height of the next row of stitches. When crocheting granny squares, you are working in rounds always from the right side and continuing in the same direction, but you still crochet a chain to begin the round. If the next round will be single crochet, you chain 1 to begin; half-double crochet: chain 2; double crochet: chain 3; triple crochet: chain 4, etc. The directions will tell you how many chains to make. The beginning chain counts as a stitch. For instance, the directions may say, ch 3 (counts as dc). At the end of each round, the last stitch is worked into the beginning chain from the previous round.

INVISIBLE JOIN

When working in the round, connecting the end of the round to the beginning can sometimes seem awkward. Here is a way to connect the last stitch in a way that will leave the connection nearly invisible. End the last stitch but do not join to the beginning with a slip stitch (1). Cut the yarn, leaving a tail several inches long. Pull the yarn through the last stitch and set the hook aside. Thread the tail on a tapestry needle, and run the needle under the beginning stitch, pulling the tail through (2). Insert the needle back through the center of the last stitch of the round and pull the tail to the back of the work (not too tightly) (3). This will join the beginning to the end invisibly (4). Weave the tail into the back of the work.

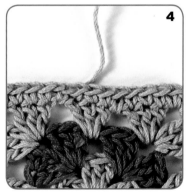

PICKING UP STITCHES FOR BORDERS

You often need to pick up stitches from the edges of a crocheted piece to add a border. If the edges are sides of granny squares, simply pick up one stitch for every stitch along the edge.

Picking up stitches along row ends of a crocheted piece is a little more complex. The general rule of thumb is to pick up one stitch in every other row for single crochet (1). For instance, if you have worked twenty rows of single crochet, you will pick up ten stitches along the row ends.

Pick up one stitch for every row for double crochet (2). For instance, if you have worked twenty rows of double crochet, you will pick up twenty stitches. These guidelines work for most people, but not all. Your work must lie flat, and sometimes you will have to experiment to judge how to proceed. If your edges are rippling, like a ruffle, you are picking up too many stitches; if they are pulling in, you are picking up too few stitches.

The best way to get an even edge is to divide the length to be worked into four parts. When the first section is done and lies flat, repeat that number of stitches for each of the following three sections. Work in every stitch of the top and bottom edges. Always work three stitches in each corner to make the project lie flat.

SEAMS

Once you have crocheted all the granny squares for a project, you join them into one large piece using one of several methods. For some methods you sew seams with yarn and a tapestry needle. For other methods, you use a crochet hook. Some might consider this final step of a project to be a chore, but to me, the rhythm of hand sewing is soothing and relaxing.

WHIPSTITCH SEAM

The whipstitch seam works best for sewing straight-edged seams. This method creates a little decorative ridge on the right side of work. Place two squares side by side, wrong side up, aligning the stitches of the outer round. Insert the needle through the top loops of corresponding stitches, bring through and around, and repeat.

wrong side

right side

WEAVE SEAM

I use this join when I want a really flat seam. Hold pieces to be seamed side by side and, working from the wrong side, insert needle from front to back, through 1 loop only, draw through, progress to next stitch, bring needle from back to front (not over), and proceed in this manner until seam is completed. If you draw through top loop only, a decorative ridge will be left on the right side of work. If you draw through bottom loops, the ridge will be on the back of the work.

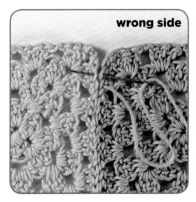

wrong side

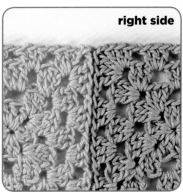

right side

right side

wrong side

SINGLE CROCHET SEAM

The single crochet seam creates a decorative ridge. Holding the pieces wrong sides together, work single crochet through the whole stitch on both motifs.

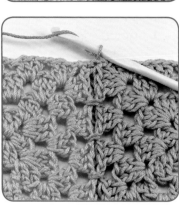

CHAIN JOIN

When the outer rounds of your squares have open spaces, you can join pieces with a stitch pattern that suits the spacing. This decorative join can be worked from either side. Place the pieces right sides together (or wrong sides together), aligning the stitches. Join yarn in one corner through both layers. *Chain 3, skip 3, single crochet through spaces of both layers, repeat from *.

GRANNY SQUARE PATTERNS

The seventy-five granny square patterns included with this book represent a small portion of the possible shapes you can crochet, but they will give you a good repertoire for designing many projects. All of the sample squares have been crocheted in the same lightweight cotton yarn with the same size hook to make the variations in the stitch patterns most apparent. As you can imagine, each of the designs will take on entirely new characteristics when you choose different colors, fibers, and weights. Play around with interesting textures and combinations from your stash and see what you can create!

SEVENTY-FIVE SQUARES

1 | PICOTS

SKILL LEVEL: Intermediate

Work stitches in chains, not in spaces.

Ch 16, join with a Sl st to form a ring.

RND 1: Ch 3 (counts as first dc), 1 dc in each of the next 3 ch, ch 7, *1 dc in each of the next 4 ch, ch 7, rep from * twice, join with a Sl st to top of beg ch-3 (4 ch-7 loops).

RND 2: Ch 5 (counts as dc, ch 2), *sk next group of dc, working in the chains of the next ch-7 loop, work [1 dc, ch 1] in each of next 7 ch, ch 1 more, rep from * twice, end with [1 dc, ch 1] in each of the next 6 ch, join with a Sl st to the 3rd ch of beg ch-5.

RND 3: Ch 1, *sc in each of next 2 ch, [1 sc next dc, ch 3, 1 sc 3rd ch from hook (picot made) sk next ch-1 sp] 6 times, 1 sc in next dc, rep from * 3 times more, join with a Sl st in the beg ch-1, fasten off.

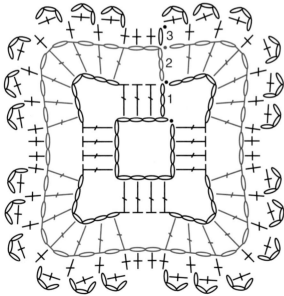

2 | DIAMOND SQUARE

SKILL LEVEL: Easy

Work the center square of this motif in rows; work second part in rounds.

Ch 6.

ROW 1: 1 sc in 2nd ch from hook, 1 sc in each ch across, turn.

ROW 2: Ch 1, 1 sc in first sc and in each sc across, turn (5 sc).

ROWS 3–6: Rep row 2.

Begin working in rounds as follows:

RND 1: Ch 1, 2 sc in first sc, 1 sc in each of next 3 sc, 3 sc in last sc (corner made), work 3 sc evenly spaced across side of square, 3 sc in corner, 1 sc in each of next 3 ch, 3 sc in corner, 3 sc evenly spaced across side, ending with 1 sc in first sc, join with Sl st to first sc (last corner completed).

RND 2: Ch 14 (counts as dc, ch 11), 1 dc in center sc of next corner, (ch 11, 1 dc in center sc of next corner) twice, ch 11, Sl st in 3rd ch of beg ch-14.

RND 3: Ch 1, 1 sc in first sc st, *15 sc in next loop, 1 sc in next dc, rep from * around, omitting last sc, join with Sl st to first sc.

RND 4: Ch 1, sk first sc, *1 sc in each of next 7 sc, 3 sc in next sc, 1 sc in each of next 7 sc, sk 1 sc, rep from * around, join with a Sl st to beg ch 1, fasten off.

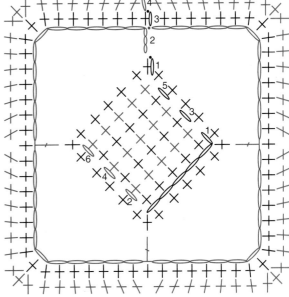

3 | ADRIENNE SQUARE

SKILL LEVEL: Easy

Ch 8, join with a Sl st to form a ring.

RND 1: Ch 1, 16 sc in ring, join with Sl st to first sc.

RND 2: Ch 7 (counts as dc, ch 4), sk next sc, *1 dc in next sc, ch 4, sk next sc, rep from * 6 times, Sl st in 3rd ch of the beg ch-7 (8 dc, 8 ch-4 sp).

RND 3: Ch 1, [1 sc, 1 hdc, 2 dc, 1 hdc, 1 sc] in each ch-4 sp around (8 petals).

RND 4: Ch 8 (counts as dc, ch 5), *1 sc between 2 dc of next petal, ch 5, 1 sc between 2 dc of next petal, ch 5**, 1 dc between the next 2 sc, ch 5, rep from * twice, rep from * to ** once, join with Sl st to 3rd ch of beg ch-8.

RND 5: Ch 3 (counts as dc), 1 dc in first st (half corner made), *[4 dc in next ch-5 sp] 3 times, [2 dc, ch 3, 2 dc] in next dc (full corner made), rep from * 3 times more, ending last rep, [2 dc, ch 3] in beg ch-3 of previous rnd, join with a Sl st to top of beg ch-3 (first corner complete), fasten off.

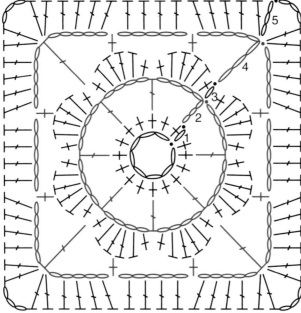

ADRIENNE HALF SQUARE

SKILL LEVEL: Easy

Worked in rows not rounds

Ch 8, join with a Sl st to form a ring.

ROW 1: 9 sc in ring, turn.

ROW 2: Ch 7 (counts as dc, ch 4) sk next sc, *1 dc in next sc, ch 4, sk next sc, rep from * 3 times, turn.

ROW 3: Ch 1, [1 sc, 1 hdc, 2 dc, 1 hdc, 1 sc] in each ch-4 sp (4 petals), turn.

ROW 4: Ch 8 (counts as dc, ch 5) *1 sc between 2 dc of next petal, ch 5, 1 sc between 2 dc of next petal, ch 5, 1 dc between next 2 sc, rep from * once, end last rep 1 dc in last sc, turn.

ROW 5: Ch 3 (counts as dc), 1 dc in first st, [4 dc in next ch-5 sp] 3 times, (2 dc, ch 3, 2 dc) in next dc, rep between [ ] 3 times, 2 dc in 3rd ch of beg ch-5, fasten off.

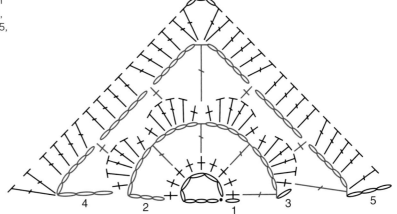

4 | CLASSIC GRANNY

SKILL LEVEL: Easy

Made with 2 colors: A and B.

With A, ch 4, join with a Sl st to form a ring.

RND 1: With A, ch 3 (counts as a dc now and throughout), 2 dc in ring, *ch 3, 3 dc in ring, rep from * twice more, ch 3, join with a Sl st to top of beg ch-3 (four groups of 3 dc), drop A.

RND 2: Join B in any corner ch-3 sp, ch 3 (counts as dc), 2 dc in same ch-3 sp, (half corner made), *ch 2, sk 3 dc, [3 dc, ch3, 3 dc] in the next ch-3 sp (corner made), rep from * twice, ch 2, 3 dc in same sp as first half corner, ch 3, join with a Sl st to top of beg ch-3, drop B.

RND 3: Pull up a loop with A in corner ch-3 loop, ch 3, 2 dc in same ch-3 sp (half corner made), *ch 2, 3 dc in next ch-2 sp, ch 2, [3 dc, ch 3, 3 dc] in next corner sp, rep from * twice, ch 2, 3 dc in next ch-2 sp, ch 2, 3 dc in same sp as first half corner, ch 3, join with a Sl st to top of beg ch-3, fasten off A.

RND 4: Pull up a loop with B in corner ch-3 loop, ch 3, 2 dc in same ch-3 space (half corner made), *[ch 2, 3 dc] in each of next 2 ch-2 sps, ch 2**, [3 dc, ch 3, 3 dc] in corner sp, rep from * twice, rep from * to ** once, 3 dc in same sp as first half corner, ch 3, join with a Sl st to beg ch-3, fasten off B.

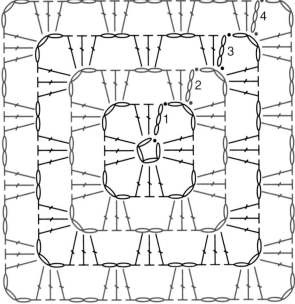

CLASSIC GRANNY HALF SQUARE

SKILL LEVEL: Easy

Made with 2 colors: A and B. Worked in rows not rounds.

With A, ch 4, join with with a Sl st to form a ring.

ROW 1: Ch 3, 3 dc in ring, ch 3, 4 dc in ring, turn, pick up a loop with B, drop A.

ROW 2: Ch 3, 3 dc in sp between the first two dc, ch 2 [3 dc, ch 3, 3 dc] in next ch-3 sp, ch 2, 3 dc in sp between last dc and tch, 1 dc in tch, pick up a loop with A, drop B, turn.

ROW 3: Ch 3, 3 dc in sp between first 2 dec, ch 2, 3 dc in next ch-2 sp, ch 2, [3 dc, ch 3, 3 dc] in next ch-3 sp, ch 2, 3 dc in next ch-2 sp, ch 2, 3 dc in sp between the last dc and tch, 1 dc in tch, pick up a loop with B, drop A, turn.

ROW 4: Ch 3, 3 dc in sp between first two dc (ch 2, 3 dc in next ch 2 sp) twice, ch 2, [3 dc, ch 3, 3 dc] in next ch-3 sp rep bet ( ) twice, ch 2, 3 dc in sp between last dc and tch, 1 dc in tch, fasten off.

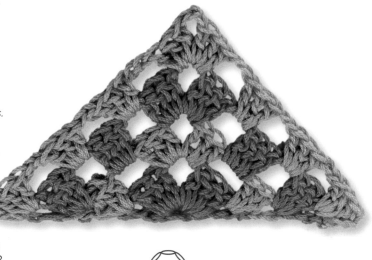

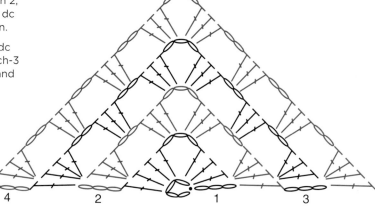

5 | NICOLE'S GRANNY

SKILL LEVEL: Easy

Ch 6, join with a Sl st to form a ring.

RND 1: Ch 3, work 2 dc in ring, (ch 1, 3 dc in ring) 3 times, ch 1, join with a Sl st to top of ch-3.

RND 2: Sl st in next 2 dc, Sl st in next ch-1 sp, ch 3, [2 dc, ch 1, 3 dc] in same ch-1 sp (corner made), *ch 1, [3 dc, ch 1, 3 dc] in next ch-1 sp, rep from * twice, ch 1, join with a Sl st to top of ch-3 (4 corners made).

RND 3: Sl st in next 2 dc, Sl st in next ch-1 corner sp, ch 3, [2 dc, ch 1, 3 dc] in same corner ch-1 sp, *ch 2, [1 dc, ch 2, 1 dc] in next ch-1 sp (V-st made), ch 2**, [3 dc, ch 1, 3 dc] in next ch-1 sp, rep from * twice, rep from * to ** once, join with Sl st to beg ch 3 (4 corners, 1 V-stitch between each corner).

RND 4: Sl st in next 2 dc, Sl st in next ch-1 corner sp, ch 3, [2 dc, ch 1, 3 dc] in same corner ch-1 sp, *ch 3, sk next ch-2 sp, [1 dc, ch 3, 1 dc] in next ch-2 sp, ch 3, sk next ch-2 sp**, [3 dc, ch 1, 3 dc] in next ch-1 sp, rep from * twice, rep from * to ** once, join with a Sl st to beg ch 3 (4 corners, 1 V-st between each corner), fasten off.

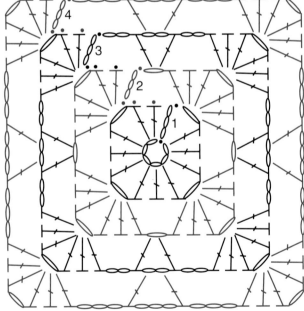

NICOLE'S GRANNY HALF SQUARE

SKILL LEVEL: Easy

Worked in rows not rounds.

Ch 6, join with a Sl st to form a ring.

ROW 1: Ch 3, work 3 dc in ring, ch 1, 4 dc in ring, ch 1, 4 dc in ring, turn.

ROW 2: Ch 3, 3 dc in sp between first 2 dc, ch 1, [3 dc, ch 1, 3 dc] in next ch-1 sp, ch 1, 3 dc in sp between last dc and tch, 1 dc in tch, turn.

ROW 3: Ch 3, 3 dc in sp between first 2 dc, ch 2 [1 dc, ch 2, 1 dc] in next ch-1 sp, ch 2 [3 dc, ch 1, 3 dc] in next ch-1 sp, ch 2, [1 dc, ch 2, 1 dc] in next ch-1 sp, ch 2, 3 dc in sp between last dc and tch, 1 dc in tch, turn.

ROW 4: Ch 3, 3 dc in sp between first two dc, *ch 3, sk next ch-2 sp, [1 dc, ch 3, 1 dc] in next ch-2 sp, ch 3, sk next ch-2 sp*, [3 dc, ch 1, 3 dc] in next ch-1 sp, rep from * to * once, 3 dc in sp between last dc and tch, 1 dc in tch, fasten off.

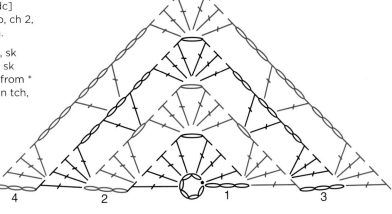

6 | JEANNINE SQUARE

SKILL LEVEL: Intermediate

Made with 4 colors: A, B, C, and D.

Double triple crochet (dtr): Yo 3 times, pick up a loop in designated place, [yo, draw through 2 loops on hook] 4 times.

With A, ch 6, join with a Sl st to form a ring.

RND 1: Ch 3 (counts as dc), 3 dc in ring, ch 3, *4 dc in ring, ch 3, rep from * twice, join with Sl st in top of beg ch-3 (4 groups of 4 dc), fasten off A.

RND 2: Join B in any ch-3 sp, ch 3, *dc in same sp, 1 dc in each of next 4 dc, 2 dc in next ch-3 sp, 1 dtr, inserting hook from front to back, going in the beg ring and between the groups of dc, 2 dc in same corner ch-3 sp, rep from * around omitting last 2 dc, join with Sl st to beg ch-3, draw C through last loop, fasten off B.

RND 3: With C, ch 3 (counts as dc), 1 dc in first st, *1 dc each next 7 dc, 2 dc in next dc, ch 3 (corner), sk next dtr**, 2 dc next dc, rep from * 2 times, rep from * to ** once, join with Sl st to top of beg ch-3, fasten off C.

RND 4: Join D in any corner ch-3 sp, ch 3, dc in same ch-3 sp, *1 dc in each of next 10 dc, 2 dc in ch-3 sp, working over ch-3 loop, 1 dtr in next dtr in rnd 2**, rep from * twice, rep from * to ** once, join with Sl st to top of beg ch-3, draw A through last loop, fasten off D.

RND 5: With A, ch 1, 1 sc in first st, 1 sc in each of next 15 sts, ch 2, *1 sc in each of next 16 sts, ch 2, rep from * twice, join with Sl st to first sc, fasten off.

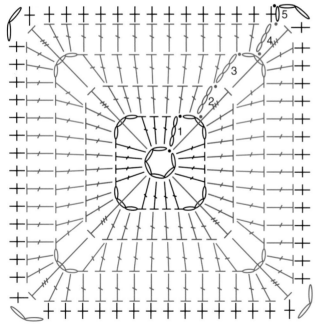

7 | RECTANGLE GRANNY

SKILL LEVEL: Intermediate

Made with 3 colors: A, B, and C.

To establish rounds, work round 1 on both sides of the foundation chain.

Beginning ch-3 always counts as first double crochet of round.

With A, ch 12.

RND 1: [2 dc, ch 2, 3 dc, ch 2, 3 dc] in 4th ch from hook, ch 2, sk next 2 ch, 1 dc in each of the next 3 ch, ch 2, sk next 2 ch, [3 dc, ch 2, 3 dc, ch 2, 3 dc] all in last ch. Working on opposite side of foundation ch, ch 2, sk next 2 ch, 1 dc in each of the next 3 ch (these 3 dc will correspond with 3 dc already established on first side of ch), ch 2, sk next 2 ch, join with a Sl st to top of beg ch-3, fasten off A.

RND 2: Join B in the last ch-2 sp made, ch 3, 2 dc in same ch-2 sp, *ch 2, [3 dc, ch 3, 3 dc, ch 2] in next 2 ch-2 sps (2 corners made), [3 dc in next ch-2 sp, ch 2] twice, rep from * once, omitting last (3 dc, ch 2), join with Sl st to top of beg ch-3, fasten off B.

RND 3: Join C in the first ch-2 sp of last rnd, ch 3, 2 dc in same ch-2 sp, ch 2, *[3 dc, ch 3, 3 dc] in next ch-2 sp (corner), ch 2, 3 dc in next ch-2 sp, ch 2, [3 dc, ch 3, 3 dc] in next ch-2 sp (corner), [ch 2, 3 dc] in each of next 3 ch-2 sps, ch 2, rep from * once, omitting last [3 dc, ch 2], join with Sl st to top of beg ch-3, fasten off C.

RND 4: Join B in the first ch-2 sp of last rnd, ch 3, 2 dc in same ch-2 sp, *ch 2, [3 dc, ch 3, 3 dc] in next ch-2 sp (corner), [ch 2, 3 dc in next ch-2 sp] twice, ch 2, [3 dc, ch 3, 3 dc] in next ch-2 sp (corner), [ch 2, 3 dc] in each of next 4 ch-2 sps, ch 2, rep from * once, omitting last [3 dc, ch 2], join with Sl st to top of beg ch-3, fasten off .

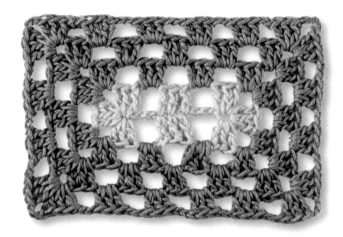

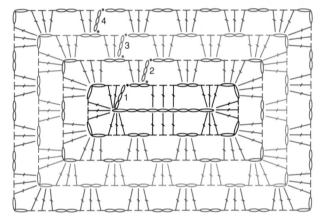

8 | BLOOMING GRANNY

SKILL LEVEL: Easy

Made with 3 colors: A, B, and C.

Popcorn (pc): Make 5 dc in specified st, draw up the last loop slightly and remove hook, insert hook in the first of the 5 dc made, pick up the dropped loop and draw it through, ch 1.

With A, ch 4, join with a Sl st to form a ring.

RND 1: With A, ch 1, 8 sc in ring, join with a Sl st in first sc.

RND 2 (PC RND): With A, ch 3 (counts as a dc), 4 dc in first st, insert hook in the top of the ch 3, pick up dropped loop, tighten, ch 1 to complete first pc, ch 1, *pc in next sc, ch 1, rep from * 6 times more, (8 pc), join with a Sl st to top of the beg ch-3, fasten off A.

RND 3: Join B in any ch-1 sp, ch 3 (counts as a dc now and throughout) 2 dc in same sp (half corner), *ch 1, 3 dc next ch-1 sp, ch 1**, [3 dc, ch 1, 3 dc] next ch-1 sp (corner), rep from * twice, rep from * to **, 3 dc in same sp as beg half corner, ch 1, join with a Sl st to top of beg ch-3 (this completes first corner), fasten off B.

RND 4: Join C in any corner ch-1 sp, ch 3, 2 dc in same sp (half corner), *[ch 1, 3 dc next ch-1 sp] twice, ch 1**, [3 dc, ch 1, 3 dc] in next ch-1 sp (corner), ch 1, rep from * twice, rep from * to ** once, 3 dc in same sp as beg half corner, ch 1, join with a Sl st to top of beg ch 3 (this completes first corner), fasten off.

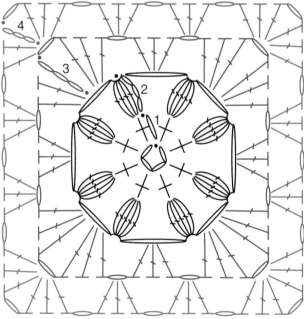

9 | LILYAN'S LACE SQUARE

SKILL LEVEL: Beginner

Ch 6, join with a Sl st to form a ring.

RND 1: Ch 3 (counts as a dc here and throughout), 15 dc in ring, join with a Sl st in 3rd ch of beg ch-3 (16 dc).

RND 2: Ch 5 (counts as a dc, ch 2), *(1 dc, ch 2) in each of next 14 dc, 1 dc in next dc, ch 1, 1 sc in 3rd ch of the beg ch-5 instead of last ch-2 sp (16 ch-2 sps).

RND 3: Ch 3, 1 dc in first sp (half corner made), *(ch 2, 1 sc) in each of next 3 ch-2 sps, ch 2, (2 dc, ch 3, 2 dc) in next ch-2 sp (corner made), rep from * twice, rep from * to ** once, 2 dc in same sp as first half corner, ch 1, hdc in 3rd ch of beg ch-3 instead of last ch-3 sp, (completes corner) (4 ch-3 corner sps).

RND 4: Ch 3, 1 dc in first sp (half corner made), *(ch 2, 1 sc) in each of next 4 ch-2 sps, ch 2**, (2 dc, ch 3, 2 dc) in next ch-3 sp (corner made), rep from * twice, rep from * to ** once, 2 dc in same sp as first half corner, ch 1, hdc in 3rd ch of beg ch-3 instead of last ch-3 sp (completes corner).

RND 5: Ch 3, 2 dc in first sp (half corner made), *(ch 1, 2 dc) in each of next 5 ch-2 sps, ch 1**, (3 dc, ch 2, 3 dc) in next corner sp, rep from * twice, rep from * to ** once, 3 dc in same sp as first half corner, ch 1, hdc in 3rd ch of beg ch 3 instead of last ch-3 sp (completes corner). Fasten off.

10 | GREAT GRANDMA'S SQUARE

SKILL LEVEL: Intermediate

Popcorn (pc): Work 5 dc in designated st, remove hook from last loop, place hook from front to back in top of the first of last 5 dc, pick up dropped loop, draw through loop on hook to complete pc.

Ch 8, join with a Sl st to form a ring.

RND 1: Ch 3 (counts as a dc here and throughout), 15 dc in ring, join with a Sl st to 3rd ch of beg ch-3 (16 dc).

RND 2: Ch 3, 2 dc in each of next 15 dc, 1 dc in first dc of rnd 1, join with a Sl st in 3rd ch of beg ch-3 (32 dc).

RND 3: Ch 3, *1 pc in next dc, 1 dc in next dc, rep from * 15 times, join with a Sl st to 3rd ch of beg ch-3 (16 pc, 16 dc).

RND 4: Ch 1, sc in first dc, *ch 2, sk next pc, 1 sc in the next dc, rep from * 15 times, ch 2, join with a Sl st in first sc (16 ch-2 sps).

RND 5: Sl st in next ch-2 sp, ch 3, 2 dc in first ch-2 sp, *ch 1, 3 dc in the next ch-2 sp, rep from * 14 times, sc in 3rd ch of beg ch-3 instead of last ch-1 sp (16 ch-1 sps).

RND 6: Ch 3, 2 dc in first sp (half corner made), *(ch 1, 3 dc) in each of next 3 ch-1 sps, ch 1**, (3 dc, ch 3, 3 dc) in next ch-1 sp (corner made), rep from * twice, rep from * to ** once, 3 dc in the same sp as first half corner, ch 1, hdc in 3rd ch of beg ch-3 instead of last ch-3 sp (completes corner) (4 ch-3 corners).

RND 7: Ch 3, 2 dc in first sp (half corner made), *(ch 1, 3 dc) in each of next 4 ch-1 sps, ch 1**, (3 dc, ch 3, 3 dc) in next ch-1 sp (corner made), rep from * twice, rep from * to ** once, 3 dc in same sp as first half corner, ch 1, hdc in 3rd ch of beg ch-3 instead of last ch-3 sp (completes corner).

RND 8: Ch 3, 2 dc in first sp (half corner made), *(ch 1, 3 dc) in each of next 5 ch-1 sps, ch 1**, (3 dc, ch 3, 3 dc) in next ch-1 sp (corner made), rep from * twice, rep from * to ** once, 3 dc in the same sp as first half corner, ch 1, hdc in 3rd ch of beg ch-3 instead of last ch-3 sp (completes corner).

RND 9: Ch 3, 2 dc in first sp (half corner made), *[1 dc in each of next 3 dc, 1 dc in next ch-1 sp] 6 times, 1 dc in each of next 3 dc**, (3 dc, ch 3, 3 dc) in next ch-3 sp (corner made), rep from * twice, rep from * to ** once, 3 dc in same sp as first half corner, ch 3, join with a Sl st in 3rd ch of beg ch-3 (completes corner).

RND 10: Ch 1, starting in same st, *1 sc in each dc across to next corner, 3 sc in next corner sp, rep from * around, join with a Sl st in first sc. Fasten off.

11 | DOGWOOD FLOWER

SKILL LEVEL: Intermediate

Double crochet 5 together (dc5tog): (Yo, draw up loop in next st, yo, draw through 2 loops on hook) 5 times, yo and draw through 6 loops on hook.

Double crochet 6 together (dc6tog): (Yo, draw up loop in next st, yo, draw through 2 loops on hook) 6 times, yo and draw through 7 loops on hook.

Ch 10, join with a Sl st to form a ring.

RND 1: Ch 3 (counts as a dc here and throughout), 4 dc in ring, [ch 7, 5 dc] 3 times in ring, ch 7, join with a Sl st in 3rd ch of beg ch-3 (4 ch-7 sps).

RND 2: Ch 3, 1 dc in next dc, *2 dc in next dc, 1 dc in each of next 2 dc, ch 2, (3 dc, ch 5, 3 dc) in next ch-7 sp (corner made), ch 2**, 1 dc in each of the next 2 dc, rep from * twice, rep from * to ** once, join with a Sl st in 3rd ch of beg ch 3 (4 ch-5 corner sps).

RND 3: Ch 2, dc5tog worked across next 5 dc, *ch 5, sk next dc, 1 dc in next dc, ch 3, (2 dc, ch 2, 2 dc) in next ch-5 sp, ch 3, sk next dc, 1 dc in next dc, ch 5, sk next dc**, dc6tog worked across next 6 dc, rep from * twice, rep from * to ** once, join with a Sl st in top of first cluster.

RND 4: Ch 1, sc in first cluster, *3 sc in next ch-5 sp, 1 sc in the next dc, 3 sc in next ch-3 sp, 1 sc in each of the next 2 dc, 3 sc in the next ch-2 sp, 1 sc in each of next 2 dc, 3 sc in next ch-3 sp, 1 sc in next dc, 3 sc in next ch-5 sp**, 1 sc in top of next cluster, rep from * twice, rep from * to ** once, join with a Sl st in first sc. Fasten off.

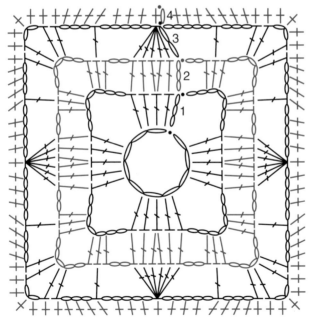

12 | LILY POND

SKILL LEVEL: Beginner

Made with 2 colors: A and B.

Double triple crochet (dtr): Yo (3 times), insert hook in next st, yo, draw up a loop, (yo, draw through 2 loops on hook) 4 times.

With A, ch 8, join with a Sl st to form a ring.

RND 1: Ch 3 (counts as a dc), 1 dc in ring, [ch 7, 2 dc] 3 times in ring, ch 7, Sl st to 3rd ch of beg ch-3 (4 ch-7 sps).

RND 2: *Ch 2, (1 sc, 1 hdc, 2 dc, 2 tr, 1 dtr, 2 tr, 2 dc, 1 hdc, 1 sc) in next ch-7 sp**, ch 2, rep from * twice, rep from * to ** once, join with a Sl st in 2nd ch of beg ch-2 (4 petals made). Fasten off A.

RND 3: With right side facing, join B with Sl st between the 2 dc of any group of 2 dc in rnd 1, ch 10 (counts as 1 dc, ch 7), *working behind sts in rnd 2, sk next petal, 1 dc between next 2 dc in rnd 1, ch 7, rep from * twice, end with Sl st in the 3rd ch of beg ch-10 (4 ch-7 sps).

RND 4: Ch 1, (1 sc, 7 dc, ch 4, 7 dc, 1 sc) in each ch-7 sp around, join with a Sl st in first sc. Fasten off B.

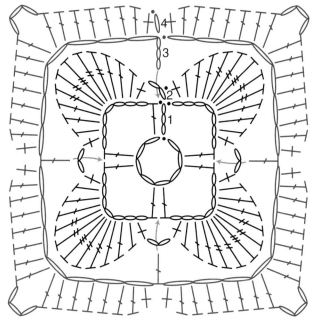

13 | CLUSTER CROSS SQUARE

SKILL LEVEL: Intermediate

Beginning cluster (beg cluster): Ch 3, [yo, insert hook in next st or sp, yo, draw up a loop, yo, draw through 2 loops on hook] twice in same st or sp, yo, draw through 3 loops on hook.

Cluster: [Yo, insert hook in next st or sp, yo, draw up a loop, yo, draw through 2 loops on hook] 3 times in same st or sp, yo, draw through 4 loops on hook.

Ch 8, join with a Sl st to form a ring.

RND 1: Work 1 beg cluster in ring, *ch 5, 1 cluster in ring, ch 2**, 1 cluster in ring, rep from * twice, rep from * to ** once, join with a Sl st to 3rd ch of beg ch-3.

RND 2: Sl st to center of next ch-5 sp, work beg cluster in first sp (half corner made), *ch 2, 3 dc in next ch-2 sp, ch 2**, (1 cluster, ch 2, 1 cluster) in next ch-5 sp (corner made), rep from * twice, rep from * to ** once, 1 cluster in same ch-5 sp as beg cluster, ch 1, sc in 3rd ch of beg ch-3 instead of last ch-3 sp (completes corner).

RND 3: Work beg cluster in first sp (half corner made), *ch 2, work 2 dc in next ch-2 sp, 1 dc in each of next 3 dc, 2 dc in next ch-2 sp, ch 2**, (1 cluster, ch 2, 1 cluster) in the next ch-2 sp (corner made), rep from * twice, rep from * to ** once, 1 cluster in same sp as beg cluster, ch 1, sc in 3rd ch of beg ch-3 instead of last ch-3 sp (completes corner).

RND 4: Work beg cluster in first sp (half corner made), *ch 2, 2 dc in next ch-2 sp, 1 dc in each of next 7 dc, 2 dc in next ch-2 sp, ch 2**, (1 cluster, ch 3, 1 cluster) in next ch-2 sp (corner made), rep from * twice, rep from * to ** once, 1 cluster in same ch-2 sp as beg cluster, ch 3, join with a Sl st in 3rd ch of beg ch-3 (completes corner). Fasten off.

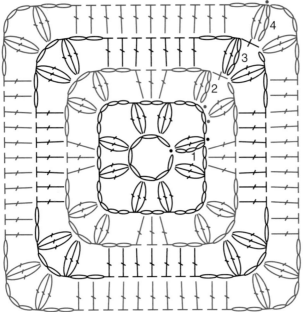

14 | CONE FLOWER

SKILL LEVEL: Intermediate

Made with 2 colors: A and B.

Beginning cluster (beg cluster): Ch 3, [yo, insert hook in next st or sp, yo, draw up a loop, yo, draw through 2 lps] twice in same st or sp, yo, draw through 3 loops on hook.

Cluster: [Yo, insert hook in next st or sp, yo, draw up a loop, yo, draw through 2 loops on hook] 3 times in same st or sp, yo, draw through 4 loops on hook.

With A, ch 5, join with a Sl st to form a ring.

RND 1: With A, ch 1, 12 sc in ring, join with a Sl st in first sc (12 sc).

RND 2: With A, *ch 15, Sl st in next sc, rep from * 11 times, working last Sl st into Sl st at end of rnd 1 (12 ch-15 loops). Fasten off A.

RND 3: With right side facing, join B in center of any ch-15 loop, ch 1, sc in first ch-15 loop, *ch 4, 1 sc in next ch-15 loop ch 4, (1 cluster, ch 4, 1 cluster) in next ch-15 loop (corner made), ch 4**, 1 sc in next ch-15 loop, rep from * twice, rep from * to ** once, join with a Sl st in first sc (16 ch-4 sps).

RND 4: With B, Sl st to center of first ch-4 sp, beg cluster in first sp, *ch 4, sc in next ch-4 sp, ch 4, (1 cluster, ch 4, 1 cluster) in next ch-4 sp (corner made), ch 4, 1 sc in next ch-4 sp, ch 4**, 1 cluster in next ch-4 sp, rep from * twice, rep from * to ** once, join with Sl st in 3rd ch of beg ch-3 (20 ch-4 sps). Fasten off.

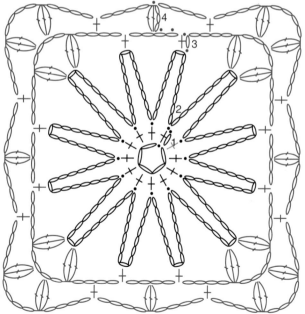

15 | BUILDING BLOCK

SKILL LEVEL: *Beginner*

Ch 10, join with a Sl st to form a ring.

RND 1: Ch 3 (counts as dc here and throughout), 3 dc in ring, [ch 7, 4 dc] 3 times in ring, ch 7, join with a Sl st in 3rd ch of beg ch-3 (4 ch-7 loops).

RND 2: Ch 1, sc in first dc, 1 sc in each of next 3 dc, *1 sc in each of next 3 ch, (1 sc, ch 2, 1 sc) in next ch, 1 sc in each of next 3 ch**, 1 sc in each of next 4 dc, rep from * twice, rep from * to ** once, join with a Sl st in first sc (4 ch-2 corner sps).

RND 3: Ch 3, 1 dc in each of next 7 sc, *(1 dc, ch 7, 1 dc) in next ch-2 sp**, 1 dc in each of next 12 sc, rep from * twice, rep from * to ** once, 1 dc in each of next 4 sc, join with Sl st in 3rd ch of beg ch-3 (4 ch-7 corner loops).

RND 4: Ch 1, sc in first dc, 1 sc in each of next 8 dc, *1 sc in each of next 3 ch, (1 sc, ch 2, 1 sc) in next ch, 1 sc in each of next 3 ch**, 1 sc in each of next 14 dc, rep from * twice, rep from * to ** once, 1 sc in each next 5 dc, join with a Sl st in first sc (4 ch-2 corner sps).

RND 5: Ch 3, 1 dc in each of next 12 sc, *3 dc in next ch-2 sp, 1 dc in each of next 22 sc, rep from * twice, rep from * to ** once, 1 dc in each of next 9 sc, join with a Sl st in 3rd ch of beg ch-3 (100 dc). Fasten off.

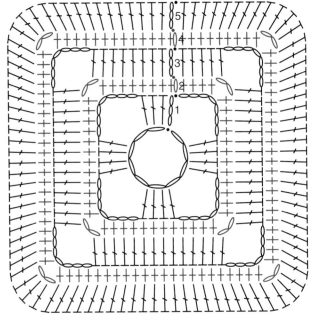

16 | BELGIAN LACE

SKILL LEVEL: Advanced Beginner

Beginning cluster (beg cluster): Ch 3, [yo, insert hook in next st or sp, yo, draw up a loop, yo, draw through 2 loops] 3 times in same st or sp, yo, draw through 3 loops on hook.

Cluster: [Yo, insert hook in next st or sp, yo, draw up a loop, yo, draw through 2 loops on hook] 4 times in same st or sp, yo, draw through 5 loops on hook.

Ch 8, join with a Sl st to form a ring.

RND 1: Ch 3 (counts as dc here and throughout), 6 dc in ring, [ch 7, 7 dc] 3 times in ring, ch 4, dc in 3rd ch of beg ch-3 instead of last ch-7 sp (4 ch-7 sps).

RND 2: Ch 10 (counts as dc, ch 7), sk next 3 dc, *1 sc in next dc, ch 7, sk next 3 dc**, 7 dc in next ch-7 sp, ch 7, sk next 3 dc, rep from * twice, rep from * to ** once, 6 dc in next ch-7 sp, join with a Sl st in 3rd ch of beg ch-10 (8 ch-7 sps).

RND 3: Sl st to center of next ch-7 sp, beg cluster in same sp, *ch 3, 1 cluster in next ch-7 sp, ch 11, sk next 3 dc, 1 dc in next dc, ch 11**, 1 cluster in next ch-7 sp, rep from * twice, rep from * to ** once, join with a Sl st in 3rd ch of beg ch-3.

RND 4: Sl st in next ch-3 sp, beg cluster in same sp, *ch 8, 7 dc in each of next 2 ch-11 sps, ch 8**, 1 cluster in next ch-3 sp, rep from * twice, rep from * to ** once, join with a Sl st in top of beg cluster.

RND 5: Ch 4 (counts as tr), 2 tr in first cluster (half corner made), *4 dc in next ch-8 sp, sk 1 dc, dc in each of next 12 dc, sk 1 dc, 4 dc in next ch-8 sp**, (3 tr, ch 3, 3 tr) in top of next cluster (corner), rep from * twice, rep from * to ** once, 3 tr in top of beg cluster in rnd 4, ch 3, join with a Sl st to 4th ch of beg ch-4 (completes corner). Fasten off.

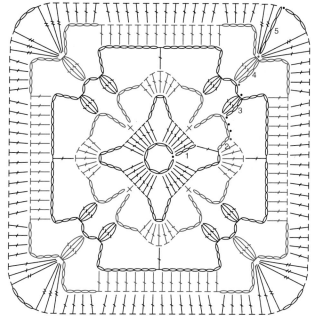

17 | BUTTERFLY GARDEN SQUARE

SKILL LEVEL: Intermediate

Tr worked 3 rounds below: Yo (twice), insert hook in 4th dc of 7 skipped sts 3 rnds below, pick up a loop catching both ch-loops on both previous rnds, [yo, draw yarn through 2 loops on hook] 3 times.

Ch 4, join with a Sl st to form a ring.

RND 1: Ch 3 (counts as dc here and throughout), 15 dc in ring, join with a Sl st in 3rd ch of beg ch-3 (16 dc).

RND 2: Ch 3, (1 dc, ch 2, 2 dc) in same st (corner made), *1 dc in each of next 3 dc**, (2 dc, ch 2, 2 dc) in next dc (corner), rep from * twice, rep from * to ** once, join with a Sl st in 3rd ch of beg ch-3 (4 ch-2 corner sps).

RND 3: Sl st in next dc and in next ch-2 sp, ch 3, (1 dc, ch 2, 2 dc) in next ch-2 sp, *ch 6, sk next 7 dc, (2 dc, ch 2, 2 dc) in next corner ch-2 sp, rep from * twice, rep from * to ** once, join with a Sl st in 3rd ch of beg ch-3 (4 ch-6 sps, 4 ch-2 sps).

RND 4: Sl st in next dc and in next ch-2 sp, ch 3, (1 dc, ch 2, 2 dc) in same sp, *dc in next 2 dc, ch 6, sk next ch-6 sp, dc in each of next 2 dc**, (2 dc, ch 2, 2 dc) in next ch-2 sp, rep from * twice, rep from * to ** once, join with a Sl st in 3rd ch of beg ch-3 (4 ch-6 sps, 4 ch-2 sps).

RND 5: Sl st in next dc and in next ch-2 sp, ch 3, (1 dc, ch 2, 2 dc) in same sp, *1 dc in each of next 4 dc, ch 3, working over ch-loops in last 2 rnds, 1 tr in 4th dc of next 7 skipped dc in rnd 2, ch 3, 1 dc in each of next 4 dc**, (2 dc, ch 2, 2 dc) in next corner ch-2 sp, rep from * twice, rep from * to ** once, join with a Sl st in 3rd ch of beg ch-3 (8 ch-3 sps, 4 ch-2 sps).

RND 6: Sl st in next dc and in next ch-2 sp, ch 1, *(1 sc, ch 2, 1 sc) in same sp, 1 sc in each of next 6 dc, 3 sc in the next ch-3 sp, 1 sc in next tr, 3 sc in next ch-3 sp, 1 sc in each of next 6 dc, rep from * around, join with a Sl st in first sc.

RND 7: Sl st in next ch-2 sp, ch 3, (1 dc, ch 2, 2 dc) in same sp, *ch 6, sk next 7 sc, 1 dc in each of next 7 sc, ch 6, sk next 7 sc**, (2 dc, ch 2, 2 dc) in next corner ch-2 sp, rep from * twice, rep from * to ** once, join with a Sl st in 3rd ch of beg ch-3.

RND 8: Sl st in the next dc and in next ch-2 sp, ch 3, (1 dc, ch 2, 2 dc) in same sp, *1 dc in each of next 2 dc, ch 6, sk next ch-6 sp, 1 dc in each of next 7 dc, ch 6, sk next ch-6 sp, 1 dc in each of next 2 dc**, (2 dc, ch 2, 2 dc) in next corner ch-2 sp, rep from * twice, rep from * to ** once, join with a Sl st in 3rd ch of beg ch-3.

RND 9: Sl st in next dc and in next ch-2 sp, ch 3, (1 dc, ch 2, 2 dc) in same sp, *1 dc in each of next 4 dc, ch 3, working over ch-loops in last 2 rnds, 1 tr in 4th sc of next 7 skipped sc in rnd 6, ch 3, 1 dc in each of next 7 dc, ch 3, working over ch-loops in last 2 rnds, 1 tr in 4th sc of 7 skipped sc in rnd 6, ch 3, 1 dc in each of next 4 dc**, (2 dc, ch 2, 2 dc) in next corner ch-2 sp, rep from * twice, rep from * to ** once, join with a Sl st in 3rd ch of beg ch-3.

RND 10: Sl st in next dc and in next ch-2 sp, ch 1, *(1 sc, ch 2, 1 sc) in corner ch-2 sp, 1 sc in each of next 6 dc, 3 sc in next ch-3 sp, 1 sc in next tr, 3 sc in next ch-3 sp, 1 sc in each of next 7 dc, 3 sc in next ch-3 sp, 1 sc in next tr, 3 sc in next ch-3 sp, 1 sc in each of next 6 dc, rep from * around, join with a Sl st in first sc. Fasten off.

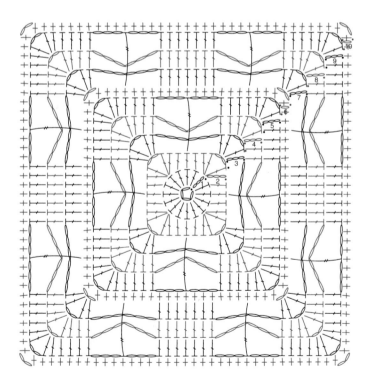

18 | TRI-COLOR CLUSTERS

SKILL LEVEL: Experienced

Made with 3 colors: A, B, and C.

Double crochet 5 together (dc5tog): (Yo, draw up loop in next st, yo, draw through 2 loops on hook) 5 times, yo and draw through 6 loops on hook.

Double crochet 6 together (dc6tog): (Yo, draw up loop in next st, yo, draw through 2 loops on hook) 6 times, yo and draw through 7 loops on hook.

On rounds 3 and 5 you will be working into sts 2 rows below.

With A, ch 8, join with a Sl st to form a ring.

RND 1: With A, ch 3 (counts as dc here and throughout), 5 dc in ring, [ch 3, 6 dc] 3 times in ring, ch 3, join with a Sl st in 3rd ch of beg ch-3 (4 ch-3 sps).

RND 2: With A, ch 3, dc5tog worked across next 5 sts, *ch 5, Sl st in 2nd ch of next ch-3 sp, ch 5**, dc6tog worked across next 6 sts, rep from * twice, rep from * to ** once, join with a Sl st to 3rd ch of beg ch-3 (4 clusters, 8 ch-5 sps), drop A to wrong side. Do not fasten off.

RND 3: With right side facing, join B in top of any cluster, *working over sts in rnd 2, work (3 dc, ch 1, 3 dc, ch 2, 3 dc, ch 1, 3 dc) in next ch-3 sp in rnd 1, Sl st in top of next cluster, rep from * 3 times more, working last Sl st in the same place as joining (4 ch-2 sps), pick up A. Fasten off B.

RND 4: With A, ch 3, 5 dc in the first st, *sk next (3 dc, ch 1, 3 dc), work (6 dc, ch 2, 6 dc) in next ch-2 sp, sk next (3 dc, ch 1, 3 dc)**, 6 dc in Sl st in top of next cluster, rep from * twice, rep from * to **, join with a Sl st in 3rd ch of beg ch-3 (4 ch-2 sps). Fasten off A.

RND 5: With right side facing, join C in last Sl st of rnd 4, ch 1, 1 sc in first dc, 1 sc in each of next 5 dc, *working over sts in rnd 4, 1 sc in next ch-1 sp between the groups of dc in rnd 3, 1 sc in each of the next 6 dc, 3 sc in next ch-2 sp, 1 sc in each of next 6 dc, working over sts in rnd 4, 1 sc in next ch-1 sp between the groups of dc in rnd 3**, 1 sc in each of next 6 dc, rep from * twice, rep from * to ** once, join with a Sl st in first sc (92 sc).

RND 6: With C, ch 3 (counts as dc), 1 dc in each of next 13 sc, *3 dc in next sc, 1 dc in each of next 22 sc; rep from * twice, 3 dc in next sc, dc in each of next 8 sc, join with a Sl st in 3rd ch of beg ch-3 (100 dc). Fasten off.

19 | VARIATION ADRIENNE SQUARE

SKILL LEVEL: Beginner

Made with 2 colors: A and B.

With A, Ch 8, join with a Sl st to form a ring.

RND 1: With A, ch 1, 16 sc in ring, join with a Sl st in first sc (16 sc).

RND 2: With A, ch 6, (counts as dc, ch 3), sk next sc, *1 dc next sc, ch 3, sk next sc, rep from * around, join with a Sl st in 3rd ch of beg ch-3 (8 ch-3 sps).

RND 3: With A, ch 1, (1 sc, 1 hdc, 2 dc, 1 hdc, 1 sc) in each ch-3 sp around, join with a Sl st in first sc (8 petals made). Fasten off A.

RND 4: With right side facing, join B between any 2 sc, ch 8 (counts as dc, ch 5), *1 sc between 2 dc of next petal, ch 5, 1 sc between 2 dc of next petal, ch 5**, 1 dc bet next 2 sc, rep from * twice, rep from * to ** once, join with a Sl st in 3rd ch of beg ch-3 (12 ch-5 sps).

RND 5: With B, ch 3 (counts as a dc), dc in same st (half corner made), *ch 1 (3 dc, ch 1) in each of next 3 ch-5 sps**, (2 dc, ch 2, 2 dc) in next dc (corner made), rep from * twice, rep from * to ** once, 2 dc in same sp as first half corner, ch 2, join with a Sl st in 3rd ch of beg ch-3 (completes corner). Fasten off B.

RND 6: With right side facing, join A in any ch-2 sp, ch 1, *(1 sc, ch 2, 1 sc) in corner ch-2 sp, 1 sc in each of next 2 dc [1 sc next sp, 1 sc in each of next 3 dc] 3 times, 1 sc next ch-1 sp, 1 sc in each of next 2 dc, rep from * around, join with a Sl st in first sc. Fasten off A.

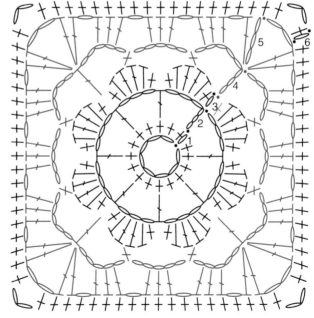

20 | DANIA SQUARE

SKILL LEVEL: Intermediate

Made with 4 colors: A, B, C, and D.

With A, ch 10, join with a Sl st to form a ring.

RND 1: With A, ch 1, 20 sc in ring, join with a Sl st in first sc (20 sc).

RND 2: With A, ch 1, *1 sc in next sc, ch 8, sk next 4 sc, rep from *around, join with a Sl st to first sc (4 ch-8 sps).

RND 3: With A, ch 1, 1 sc in first sc, *(4 sc, ch 3, 4 sc) in next ch-8 sp**, 1 sc in next sc, rep from * twice, rep from * to ** once, join with a Sl st in first sc (36 sc, 4 ch-3 sps). Fasten off A.

RND 4: With right side facing, join B in any ch-3 sp, ch 1, 1 sc in same sp (half corner made), *1 sc in each of next 9 sc**, (1 sc, ch 2, 1 sc) in next ch-2 sp, rep from * twice, rep from * to ** once, 1 sc in same ch-2 sp as first half corner, ch 2, join with a Sl st in first sc (completes corner) (4 ch-2 sps). Fasten off B.

RND 5: With right side facing, join C in any ch-2 corner sp, ch 1, 1 sc in same sp (half corner made), *1 sc in each of next 11 sc**, (1 sc, ch 2, 1 sc) in next ch-2 sp, rep from * twice, rep from * to ** once, 1 sc in same ch-2 sp as first half corner, ch 2, join with a Sl st in first sc (completes corner). Fasten off C.

THE GRANNY SQUARE BOOK

RND 6: With right side facing, join D in any ch-2 corner sp, ch 5 (counts as 1 dc, ch 2), 1 dc in same sp (corner made), *1 dc in each of next 13 sc**, (1 dc, ch 2, 1 dc) in corner ch-2 sp, rep from * twice, rep from * to ** once, join with a Sl st in 3rd ch of beg ch-5. Fasten off D.

RND 7: With right side facing, join A in any corner ch-2 sp, ch 5, 1 dc in same sp (corner made), *[ch 1, sk 1 dc, 1 dc in next dc] 7 times, ch 1**, (1 dc, ch 2, 1 dc) in next ch-2 sp, rep from * twice, rep from * to ** once, join with a Sl st to 3rd ch of beg ch-5 (32 ch-1 sps, 4 ch-2 sps).

RND 8: With A, Sl st in next ch-2 sp, ch 1, *(2 sc, ch 2, 2 sc) in ch-2 corner sp, 2 sc in each of next 8 ch-1 sps, rep from * 3 times, join with a Sl st to first sc (80 sc, 4 ch-2 sps). Fasten off A.

RND 9: With right side facing, join B in any corner ch-2 sp, ch 5, 1 dc in same sp (corner made), *[ch 1, sk next sc, 1 dc next sc] 10 times, ch 1**, (1 dc, ch 2, 1 dc) in next ch-2 sp, rep from * twice, rep from * to ** once, join with a Sl st in 3rd ch of beg ch-5 (44 ch-1 sps, 4 ch-2 sps). Fasten off B.

RND 10: With right side facing, join C in any corner ch-2 sp, ch 1, *(2 sc, ch 2, 2 sc) in corner ch-2 sp, 2 sc in each of next 11 ch-1 sps, rep from * 3 times, join with a Sl st to first sc. Fasten off C.

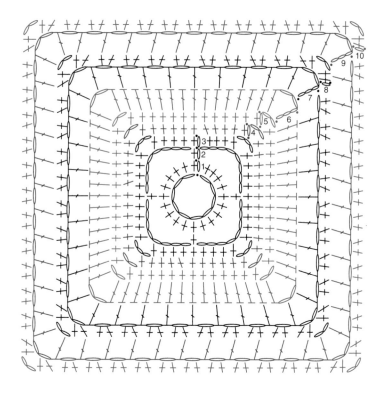

21 | PETITE FLOWER

SKILL LEVEL: Intermediate

Made with 2 colors: A and B.

Cluster: [Yo (twice), draw up a loop in next st, (yo, draw through 2 loops on hook) twice] twice, yo, draw through all 3 loops on hook.

With A, ch 4, join with a Sl st to form a ring.

RND 1: With A, ch 4, 1 tr in ring (counts as first cluster), ch 3, [1 cluster, ch 3] 7 times in ring, join with a Sl st in 4th ch of beg ch-4 (8 clusters). Fasten off A.

RND 2: With right side facing, join B in any ch-3 sp, ch 1, 1 sc same sp, *(ch 5, 1 sc) in each of next 7 ch-3 sps, ch 5, join with a Sl st in first sc (8 ch-5 sps).

RND 3: With B, Sl st in first 3 ch sts of next ch-5 sp, ch 4 (counts as dc, ch 1), *[1 cluster, ch 1] 5 times in next ch-5 sp**, 1 dc in next ch-5 sp, ch 1, rep from * twice, then rep from * to ** once, join with a Sl st to 3rd ch of beg ch-4 (24 ch-1 sps).

RND 4: With B, ch 4 (counts as tr), 1 tr in same st (half corner made), ch 1, *(1 dc, ch 1) in each of next 4 ch-1 sps**, (2 tr, ch 2, 2 tr) in next tr (corner made), rep from * twice, rep from * to ** once, 2 tr in same sp as first half corner, ch 2, join with a Sl st in 3rd ch of beg ch-3 (completes corner). Fasten off B.

22 | FORGET ME NOT

SKILL LEVEL: Intermediate

Made with 2 colors: A and B.

Beginning cluster (beg cluster): Ch 3, [yo, insert hook in st or sp, yo, draw up a loop, yo, draw through 2 loops] twice in same st or sp, yo, draw through 3 loops on hook.

Cluster: [Yo, insert hook in st or sp, yo, draw up a loop, yo, draw through 2 loops on hook] 3 times in same st or sp, yo, draw through 4 loops on hook.

With A, ch 5, join with a Sl st to form a ring.

RND 1: With A, ch 1, 8 sc in ring, join with a Sl st in first sc (8 sc).

RND 2: With A, beg cluster in first sc, ch 2, (cluster, ch 2) in each sc around, join with a Sl st in 3rd ch of beg ch-3 (8 clusters). Fasten off A.

RND 3: With right side facing, join B in any ch-2 sp, ch 1, 3 sc in each ch-3 sp around, join with a Sl st to first sc (24 sc).

RND 4: With B, Sl st in next sc, ch 3 (counts as dc here and throughout), 2 dc in first sc (corner), *ch 2, sk next sc, 1 dc in next sc, ch 1, sk next sc, 1 dc in next sc, ch 2, sk next sc**, 3 dc in next sc (corner), rep from * twice, rep from * to ** once, join with a Sl st in 3rd ch of beg ch-3 (8 ch-2 sp, 4 ch-1 sps).

RND 5: With B, ch 3, 1 dc between first 2 sts, ch 3, 2 dc between next 2 dc (corner made) *[ch 1, sk next ch-sp, 1 dc in next dc] twice, ch 1, sk next ch-2 sp**, 2 dc between next 2 dc, ch 3, 2 dc between next 2 dc (corner made) rep from * twice, rep from * to ** once, join with Sl st in 3rd ch of beg ch-3 (12 ch-1 sp, 4 ch-3 sps).

RND 6: With B, ch 3, 2 dc bet first 2 sts, *ch 3, sk next ch-3 sp, 3 dc bet next 2 dc, *[ch 1, sk next ch-1 sp, 1 dc in next dc] twice, ch 1, 3 dc bet next 2 dc, rep from * 3 times, rep from * to ** once, join with a Sl st to 3rd ch of beg ch-4. Fasten off B.

RND 7: With right side facing, join A in any ch-3 sp, ch 3, (2 dc, ch 3, 3 dc) in same sp, *1 sc each of next 3 dc, [1 sc next ch-1 sp, 1 sc in next dc] 3 times, 1 sc in each of next 2 dc**, (3 dc, ch 3, 3 dc) in next ch-3 sp (corner), rep from * twice, rep from * to ** once, join with a Sl st in 3rd ch of beg ch-3. Fasten off A.

23 | FERRIS WHEEL

SKILL LEVEL: Beginner

Ch 8, join with a Sl st to form a ring.

RND 1: Ch 3 (counts as dc here and throughout), 15 dc in ring, join with a Sl st in 3rd ch of beg ch-3.

RND 2: Ch 5 (counts as 1 dc, ch 2), (1 dc, ch 2) in each dc around, join with a Sl st in 3rd ch of beg ch-5 (16 ch-2 sps).

RND 3: Sl st in first ch-2 sp, ch 3, 2 dc in same sp, ch 1, (3 dc, ch 1) in each ch-2 sp around, join with a Sl st in 3rd ch of beg ch-3 (16 ch-1 sps).

RND 4: Sl st to first ch-1 sp, ch 1, sc in same sp, *(ch 3, 1 sc) in each of next 3 sps, ch 6**, 1 sc in next sp, rep from * twice, rep from * to ** once, join with a Sl st in first sc (12 ch-3 sps, 4 ch-6 sps).

RND 5: Sl st in first ch-3 sp, ch 3, 2 dc in same sp, 3 dc in each of next 2 ch-3 sps, *(5 dc, ch 3, 5 dc) in next ch-6 sp**, 3 dc in each of next 3 ch-3 sps, rep from * twice, rep from * to ** once, join with a Sl st in 3rd ch of beg ch-3 (76 dc, 4 ch-3 sps).

RND 6: Ch 3, *1 dc in each dc to corner, (1 dc, ch 3, 1 dc) in next ch-2 sp, rep from * around, 1 dc in each dc to end, join with a Sl st in 3rd ch of beg ch-3 (82 dc, 4 ch-3 sps). Fasten off.

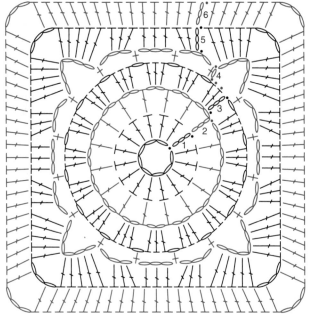

24 | CELTIC FLOWER

SKILL LEVEL: Beginner

Ch 5, join with a Sl st to form a ring.

RND 1: Ch 1, *(1 sc, ch 1, 5 dc) in ring, ch 1, rep from * 3 times, join with a Sl st in first sc (4 petals).

RND 2: Sl st to first ch-1 sp, Sl st in each of next 2 dc, ch 1, 1 sc in same st, *ch 10, 1 sc in center dc of next petal, rep from *twice, ch 10, join with a Sl st in first sc (4 ch-1 sps).

RND 3: Ch 1, *15 sc in next ch-10 sp, Sl st in next sc, rep from * around, join with a Sl st in first sc (60 sc).

RND 4: Sl st in each of the next 2 sc, ch 1, starting in same sc, *1 sc in each of the 9 sc, ch 5, sk next 6 sc, rep from * 3 times, join with a Sl st in first sc (4 ch-5 sps).

RND 5: Ch 1, sk first sc, *1 sc in each of next 7 sc, ch 5, (1 dc, ch 5, 1 dc) in 3rd ch of next ch-5 sp, ch 5, sk next sc, rep from * 3 times, join with a Sl st in first sc (12 ch-5 sps). Fasten off.

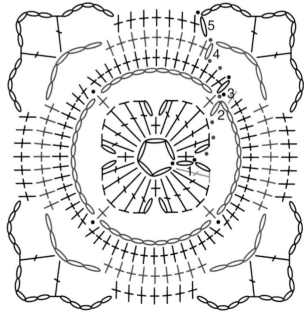

25 | FILET MESH SQUARE I

SKILL LEVEL: Intermediate

Center of square is worked in rows, then continues in rounds.

Ch 12.

ROW 1: 1 dc in 6th ch from hook, *ch 1, sk next ch, 1 dc in next ch, rep from * twice, turn (4 ch-1 sps).

ROWS 2–4: Ch 4 (counts as 1 dc ch 1), sk next ch-1 sp, (1 dc, ch 1) in each of next 3 dc, sk next ch, 1 dc next ch, turn.

Work now progresses in rnds, working along top, sides and bottom of first 4 rows.

RND 5: Ch 1, 2 sc in first ch-1 sp (half corner), [1 sc in next dc, 1 sc in next ch-1 sp] twice, 1 sc in next dc, *(2 sc, ch 2, 2 sc) in next corner sp, 5 sc worked across next 2 row-end sts*, (2 sc, ch 2, 2 sc) in next corner sp, working across opposite side of foundation ch, [1 sc in next ch at base of dc, 1 sc in next ch-1 sp] twice, 1 sc in next ch at base of dc, rep from * to * once, 2 sc in last row-end st, ch 1, sc in first sc to join instead of last ch-2 sp (completes corner) (9 sc across each side, 4 ch-2 corner sps).

RND 6: Ch 3 (counts as 1 dc here and throughout), 1 dc in same sp (half corner made), *ch 4, sk next 4 sc, 1 dc in next sc, ch 4, sk next 4 dc**, (2 dc, ch 2, 2 dc) in next ch-2 corner sp, rep from * twice, rep from * to ** once, 2 dc in same sp as first half corner, ch 1, sc in 3rd ch of beg ch-3 instead of last ch-2 sp (completes corner) (8 ch-4 sps, 4 ch-2 corner sps).

RND 7: Ch 3, 2 dc same sp (half corner made), *ch 4, sk next ch-4 sp, 3 dc in next dc, ch 4, sk next ch-4 sp**, (3 dc, ch 3, 3 dc) in next ch-2 sp (corner made), rep from * twice, rep from * to ** once, 3 dc in same sp as beg half corner, ch 1, hdc in 3rd ch of beg ch-3 instead of last ch-3 sp (completes corner) (8 ch-4 sps, 4 ch-3 corner sps).

RND 8: Ch 3, 2 dc in same sp (half corner made), *ch 2, 1 dc in next ch-4 sp, ch 2, 1 dc in next dc, ch 2, sk next dc, 1 dc next dc, ch 2, 1 dc next ch-4 sp, ch 2**, (3 dc, ch 3, 3 dc) in next corner sp, rep from * twice, rep from * to ** once, 3 dc in same sp as beg half corner, ch 3, join with a Sl st in 3rd ch of beg ch-3 (corner completed) (16 ch-2 sps, 4 ch-3 corner sps). Fasten off.

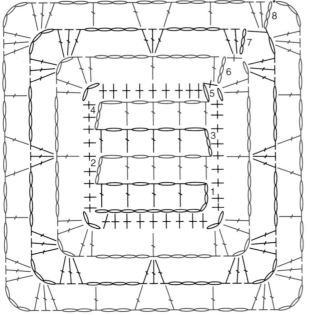

26 | FILET MESH SQUARE II

SKILL LEVEL: Intermediate

Ch 6, join with a Sl st to form a ring.

RND 1: Ch 3 (counts as dc here and throughout), 2 dc in ring, [ch 2, 3 dc] 3 times in ring, ch 1, sc in 3rd ch of beg ch-3 (4 groups of 3 dc, 4 sps).

RND 2: Ch 3, 1 dc same sp (half corner made), *2 dc in next dc, 1 dc next dc, 2 dc in next dc, (2 dc, ch 3, 2 dc) in next ch-2 sp, (1 dc, ch 1) in each of next 2 dc, 1 dc next dc*, (2 dc, ch 3, 2 dc) in next ch-3 sp, rep from * to * once, 2 dc in same sp as first half corner, ch 1, hdc in 3rd ch of beg ch-3 instead of last ch-3 sp (completes corner) (9 dc on 2 sides, 7 dc and 2 ch-1 sps on 2 sides, 4 ch-3 corner sps).

RND 3: Ch 3, 1 dc same sp (half corner made), *1 dc next dc, 2 dc in next dc, 1 dc in each of next 5 dc, 2 dc next dc, 1 dc in next dc, (2 dc, ch 3, 2 dc) in next ch-3 sp (corner made), ch 1, sk next dc, 1 dc in next dc, [ch 1, 1 dc in next dc] 3 times, ch 1, sk next dc, 1 dc in next dc, ch 1*, (2 dc, ch 3, 2 dc) in next ch-3 sp (corner), rep from * to * once, 2 dc in same sp as first half corner, ch 1, hdc in 3rd ch of beg ch-3 instead of last ch-3 sp (completes corner) (15 dc on 2 sides, 9 dc and 6 ch-1 sps on 2 sides, 4 corner ch-3 sps).

RND 4: Ch 3, 1 dc in same sp (half corner made), *1 dc next dc, 2 dc in next dc, 1 dc in each of next 11 dc, 2 dc next dc, 1 dc in next dc, (2 dc, ch 3, 2 dc) in next ch-3 sp (corner made), [ch 1, 1 dc in next dc] 8 times, ch 1, sk next dc*, (2 dc, ch 3, 2 dc) in next ch-3 sp (corner made), rep from * to * once, 2 dc in same sp as first half corner, ch 1, hdc in 3rd ch of beg ch-3 instead of last ch-3 sp (completes corner) (21 dc on 2 sides, 12 dc and 9 ch-1 sps on 2 sides, 4 corner ch-3 sps).

RND 5: Ch 3, 1 dc in same sp (half corner made), *1 dc next dc, 2 dc in next dc, 1 dc in each of next 17 dc, 2 dc next dc, 1 dc in next dc, (2 dc, ch 3, 2 dc) in next ch-3 sp (corner made), [ch 1, 1 dc in next dc] 11 times, ch 1, sk next dc*, (2 dc, ch 3, 2 dc) in next ch-3 sp (corner made), rep from * to * once, 2 dc in same sp as first half corner, ch 3, join with a Sl st in 3rd ch of beg ch-3 (completes corner) (27 dc on 2 sides, 15 dc and 12 ch-1 sps on 2 sides, 4 corner ch-3 sps). Fasten off.

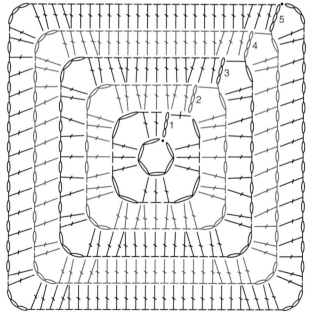

27 | FRONT POST DOUBLE CROCHET SQUARE

SKILL LEVEL: Beginner

Made with 2 colors: A and B.

Do not end colors at the end of each round, carry up on wrong side of work.

Front post double crochet (FPdc): Yo, insert hook from front to back to front again around the post of next st, yo, draw up a loop (3 loops on hook), [yo, draw yarn through 2 loops on hook] twice.

With A, ch 6, join with a Sl st to form a ring.

RND 1: With A, ch 3, (counts as 1 dc now and throughout), 2 dc in ring, [ch 3, 3 dc] 3 times in ring, ch 1, hdc in 3rd ch of the beg ch-3 instead of last ch-3 sp, drop A to wrong side, draw B through loop on hook to join (4 groups of 3 dc).

RND 2: With B, ch 3, 2 dc in first sp (half corner made), *1 FPdc in each of next 3 dc**, (3 dc, ch 3, 3 dc) in next ch-3 sp (corner made), rep from * twice, rep from * to ** once, 3 dc, in same sp as first half corner, ch 1, hdc in 3rd ch of beg ch-3 instead of last ch-3 sp (completes corner), drop B to wrong side, pick up A through loop on hook.

RND 3: With A, ch 3, 2 dc in first sp (half corner made), *1 dc in each of next 3 dc, 1 FPdc in each of next 3 dc, 1 dc in each of next 3 dc**, (3 dc, ch 3, 3 dc) in next ch-3 sp (corner made), rep from * twice, rep from * to** once, 3 dc in same sp as first half corner, ch 1, hdc in 3rd ch of beg ch-3 instead of last ch-3 sp (completes corner), drop A to wrong side, pick up B through loop on hook.

RND 4: With B, ch 3, 2 dc in first sp (half corner made), *1 dc in each of next 6 dc, 1 FPdc in each of next 3 dc, 1 dc in each of next 6 dc**, (3 dc, ch 3, 3 dc) in next ch-3 sp (corner made), rep from * twice, rep from * to ** once, 3 dc in same corner ar first half corner, ch 3, join with a Sl st to 3rd ch of beg ch-3 (completes corner). Fasten off B, draw up A through loop on hook.

RND 5: With A, ch 1, starting in same dc, *1 sc in each of next 21 dc, (2 sc, ch 2, 2 sc) in next ch-3 sp, rep from * around, join with a Sl st to first sc. Fasten off A.

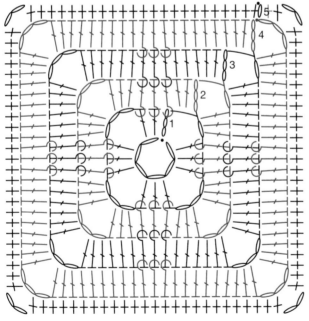

28 | PAULA'S PENDANT

SKILL LEVEL: Experienced

Made with 5 colors: A, B, C, D, and E.

With A, ch 4, join with a Sl st to form a ring.

RND 1: With A, ch 3 (counts as dc here and throughout), 1 dc in ring, [ch 1, 2 dc] 5 times in ring, ch 1, join with a Sl st in 3rd ch of beg ch-3 (6 ch-1 sps). Fasten off A.

RND 2: With right side facing, join B in any ch-1 sp, ch 3, (1 dc, ch 1, 2 dc) in same sp, (2 dc, ch 1, 2 dc) in each ch-1 sp around, join with a Sl st in 3rd ch of beg ch-3 (6 shells). Fasten off B.

RND 3: With right side facing, join C in any ch-1 sp, ch 3, 6 dc in same sp, 7 dc in each ch-1 sp around, join with a Sl st to 3rd ch of beg ch-3 (6 shells). Fasten off C.

RND 4: With right side facing, join D in first dc of any shell, starting in same st, *1 sc in each of next 7 dc, working over sts in rnd 3, 1 dc in the sp between 2 shells in rnd 2, rep from * 5 times, join with a Sl st in first sc (42 sc). Fasten off D.

RND 5: With right side facing, join E in first st, ch 1, starting in same st, 1 sc in each of next 7 sc, *(1 dc, ch 2, 1 dc) in next dc (corner made)**, 1 sc in each of next 11 sc, rep from * twice, rep from * to ** once, 1 sc in each of next 4 sc, join with a Sl st in first sc (44 sc, 8 dc, 4 ch-2 sps).

RND 6: With E, ch 1, starting in same st, 1 sc in each on next 5 sc, 1 hdc in each of next 4 sc, *(2 dc, ch 3, 2 dc) in next ch-2 sp (corner made), 1 hdc in each of next 4 sc**, 1 sc in each next 5 sc, 1 hdc in ea of next 4, rep from * twice, rep from * to ** once, 1 sc in next sc, join with a Sl st to first sc (17 sts across each side, 4 ch-3 corner sps).

RND 7: Ch 3, 1 dc in each next 9 sts, *(2 dc, ch 3, 2 dc) in next ch-3 sp (corner)**, 1 dc in each of next 17 sts, rep from * twice, rep from * to **, 1 dc in each of next 7 sts, join with a Sl st in 3rd ch of beg ch-3 (21 dc across each side, 4 ch-3 sps). Fasten off.

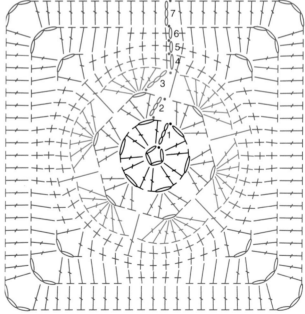

29 | FRANCES FLOWER

SKILL LEVEL: Intermediate

Made with 3 colors: A, B, and C.

With A, ch 4, join with a Sl st to form a ring.

RND 1: With A, ch 3 (counts as dc here and throughout), 2 dc in ring, [ch 3, 3 dc] 3 times in ring, ch 3, join with a Sl st to 3rd ch of beg ch-3 (4 ch-3 sps). Fasten off A.

RND 2: With right side facing, join B in any ch-3 sp, ch 3, (2 dc, ch 3, 3 dc) in same sp, ch 2, (3 dc, ch 3, 3 dc, ch 2) in each ch-3 sp around, join with a Sl st to 3rd ch of beg ch-3. Fasten off B.

RND 3: With right side facing, join C in any ch-3 corner sp, ch 3, 2 dc in same sp (half corner), *ch 2, 3 dc in next ch-2 sp, ch 2**, (3 dc, ch 3, 3 dc) in next ch-3 sp (corner), rep from * twice, rep from * to ** once, 3 dc in same sp as first half corner, ch 2, sc in 3rd ch of beg ch-3 instead of last ch-3 sp (completes corner).

RND 4: With C, ch 1, sc in same sp, *(ch 4, 1 sc) in next 2 ch-2 sp, ch 4**, (1 sc, ch 8, 1 sc) in next ch-3 sp, rep from * twice, rep * to ** once, 1 sc in same sp as first sc, ch 8, join with a Sl st to first sc (12 ch-4 sps, 4 ch-8 sps).

RND 5: With C, Sl st in next 2 ch sts, ch 1, sc in same sp, *(ch 4, sc) in each of next ch-4 sps, ch 4, (1 sc, ch 2, 1 sc) in next ch-8 sp, ch 4**, 1 sc in next ch-4 sp, rep from * twice, rep from * to ** once, join with a Sl st in first sc (16 ch-4 sps, 4 ch-2 sps).

RND 6: With C, Sl st in next 2 ch, ch 3, 1 dc in same ch-4 sp, (ch 2, 2 dc) in each of next 2 ch-4 sps, *7 dc in next ch-2 sp, 2 dc in next ch-4 sp, ch 2**, 2 dc in next ch-4 sp, rep from * twice, rep from * to ** once, join with a Sl st in 3rd ch of beg ch-3. Fasten off C.

RND 7: With right side facing, join A in first dc, ch 1, 1 sc in first 2 dc, *[2 sc in next ch-2 sp, 1 sc in each of next 2 dc] twice, 1 sc in each of next 3 dc, (1 sc, ch 2, 1 sc) in next dc, 1 sc in each of next 5 dc**, [2 sc in next ch-2 sp, 1 sc in each of next 2 dc] twice, rep from * twice, rep from * to ** once, 2 sc in next ch-2 sp, join with a Sl st in first sc. Fasten off A.

RND 8: With right side facing, join B in first sc, ch 1, starting in same st, 1 sc in each of next 14 sc, *(1 sc, ch 2, 1 sc) in next ch-2 sp**, 1 sc in each of next 22 sc, rep from * twice, rep from * to ** once, 1 sc in each of next 8 sc, join with a Sl st in first sc. Fasten off.

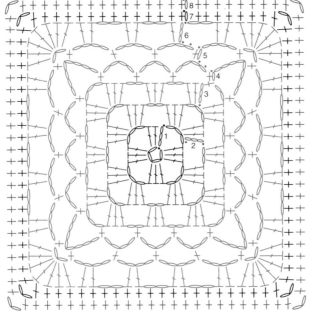

30 | SWIRLING SPIRAL

SKILL LEVEL: Experienced

Ch 5, join with a Sl st to form a ring.

RND 1: *Ch 3, 3 sc in ring, rep from * 3 times, do not join. Work in a spiral. Place marker in last sc of rnd and move marker up as work progresses.

RND 2: *Ch 4, 2 sc in next ch-3 sp, 1 sc in each of the first 2 sc, sk next sc, rep from * 3 times.

RND 3: *Ch 4, 2 sc in next ch-4 sp, 1 sc in each of next 3 sc, sk next sc, rep from * 3 times.

RND 4: *Ch 4, 2 sc in next ch-4 sp, 1 sc in each of next 4 sc, sk next sc, rep from * 3 times.

RND 5: *Ch 4, 2 sc in next ch-4 sp, 1 sc in each of next 5 sc, sk next sc, rep from * 3 times.

RND 6: *Ch 4, 2 sc in next ch-4 sp, 1 sc in each of next 6 sc, sk next sc, rep from * 3 times.

RND 7: *Ch 5, 2 sc in next ch-4 sp, 1 sc in each of next 7 sc, sk next sc, rep from * 3 times.

RND 8: *Ch 5, 2 sc in next ch-4 sp, 1 sc in each of next 8 sc, sk next sc, rep from * 3 times.

RND 9: *Ch 5, 2 sc in next ch-4 sp, 1 sc in each of next 9 sc, sk next sc, rep from * 3 times.

RND 10: *Ch 5, 2 sc in next ch-5 sp, 1 sc in each of next 10 sc, sk next sc, rep from * 3 times.

RND 11: *Ch 5, 2 sc in next ch-5 sp, 1 sc in each of next 11 sc, sk next sc, rep from * 3 times.

RND 12: *Ch 8, sk next ch-5 sp and next 2 sc, 1 sc in each of next 10 sc, sk next sc, rep from * 3 times.

RND 13: *Ch 4, (1 sc, ch 4, 1 sc) in next ch-8 sp, ch 4, sk next 2 sc, 1 sc in each of next 7 sc, sk next sc, rep from * 3 times.

RND 14: *Ch 4, 1 sc in next ch-4 sp, ch 4, (1 sc, ch 4, 1 sc) in next ch-4 sp (corner), ch 4, 1 sc in next ch-4 sp, ch 4, sk next 2 sc, 1 sc in each of next 4 sc, sk next sc, rep from * 3 times.

RND 15: *4 sc in each of next 2 ch-4 sps, (3 sc, ch 2, 3 sc) in next ch-4 sp (corner), 4 sc in each of next 2 ch-4 sps, 1 sc in each of next 4 sc, rep from * 3 times, Sl st in next sc to join. Fasten off.

31 | IRISH ROSE

SKILL LEVEL: Intermediate

Made with 2 colors: A and B.

With A, ch 6, join with a Sl st to form a ring.

RND 1: With A, ch 5 (counts as dc, ch 2), [1 dc, ch 2] 7 times in ring, join with a Sl st in 3rd ch of beg ch-5 (8 ch-2 sps).

RND 2: With A, ch 1, [1 sc, 1 dc, 1 tr, 1 dc, 1 sc] in each ch-2 sp around, turn (8 petals).

RND 3: With wrong side facing and A, ch 1, 1 sc in next dc in rnd 1, *ch 3, working behind sts in rnd 2, 1 sc in next dc in rnd 1, rep from * 6 times, ch 3, join with a Sl st in first sc, turn (8 ch-3 sps).

RND 4: With right side facing and A, ch 1, (1 sc, 2 dc, 1 tr, 2 dc, 1 sc) in each ch-3 sp around, join with a Sl st in first sc, turn (8 petals).

RND 5: With wrong side facing and A, *ch 4, working behind rnd 4, Sl st in next sc in rnd 3, rep from * around, join with a Sl st in first ch of beg ch-4, turn (8 ch-4 sps).

RND 6: With right side and A, ch 1, (1 sc, 2 dc, 3 tr, 2 dc, 1 sc) in each ch-4 sp around, join with a Sl st in first sc. Fasten off A.

RND 7: With right side facing, join B in center tr of any petal, ch 1, 1 sc in same tr, *ch 5, 1 sc in center tr of next petal, ch 14**, 1 sc in tr of next petal, rep from * twice, rep from * to ** once, join with a Sl st in first sc.

RND 8: With B, 1 sc in each ch and in each sc around, join with a Sl st in first sc, (84 sc). Fasten off B.

RND 9: With right side facing, join A in first sc, ch 3 (counts as dc), 1 dc in each of next 12 sc, *(1 dc, ch 3, 1 dc) in next sc (corner made)**, 1 dc in each of next 20 sc, rep from * twice, rep from * to ** once, 1 dc in each of next 7 sc, join with a Sl st in 3rd ch of beg ch-3. Fasten off A.

RND 10: With right side facing, join B in first dc, ch 1, starting in same st, 1 sc in each of next 14 dc, *(2 sc, ch 3, 2 sc) in next ch-3 sp (corner)**, 1 sc in each of next 22 dc, rep from * twice, rep from * to ** once, 1 sc in each of next 8 dc, join with a Sl st in first sc. Fasten off.

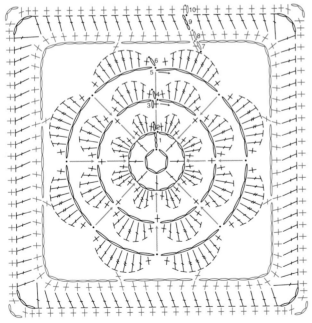

32 | BLOCK STITCH FLOWER

SKILL LEVEL: Experienced

Made with 3 colors: A, B, and C.

Block stitch: Working over the bar of the last dc just made yo and pick up a loop 4 times (9 loops on hook), pick up a loop in same sp, yo, draw through all 10 loops on hook, holding this last loop on hook, pick up a loop in same sp, ch 2, yo, draw through both loops remaining on hook (the ch-2 just made counts as the dc completing the block stitch cluster).

With A, ch 6, join with a Sl st to form a ring.

RND 1: With A, ch 5 (counts as dc, ch 2), [1 dc, ch 2] 7 times in ring, Sl st in 3rd ch of beg ch-5 (8 ch-2 sps). Fasten off A.

RND 2: With right side facing, join B in any ch-2 sp, ch 3 (counts as a dc here and throughout), 1 dc in same ch-2 sp, work block stitch over last dc just made (block st cluster made), [2 dc, block st] in each ch-2 space around, join with a Sl st in 3rd ch of beg ch-3 (8 block stitch clusters made). Fasten off B.

RND 3: Join C with a Sl st in any space between 2 dc (one dc is conventional dc, 1 dc is created by the ch-2 at end of block st cluster), *ch 5, 1 sc in next sp between 2 dc, rep from * 7 times more, join with a Sl st to beg Sl st (8 ch-5 spaces).

RND 4: With C, ch 1, sc in first sc, *ch 4, 1 sc in 3rd ch of next ch-5 sp, ch 4, 1 sc in next sc, ch 8, sk next ch-5 sp**, 1 sc in next sc, rep from * twice, rep from * to ** once, join with a Sl st in first sc.

RND 5: With C, Sl st in next ch-4 sp, ch 3, 1 dc in same sp, ch 2, 2 dc in next ch-4 sp, ch 2, *(3 dc, ch 3, 3 dc) in next ch-8 sp (corner)**, (ch 2, 2 dc) in each of next 2 ch-4 sps, rep from * twice, rep from * to ** once, ch 2, join with a Sl st in 3rd ch of beg ch-3.

RND 6: With C, Sl st in next dc and next ch-2 sp, ch 3, dc in same sp, *ch 2, 2 dc in next ch-2 sp, ch 2, (5 dc, ch 3, 5 dc) in next ch-3 sp (corner), ch 2, 2 dc in next ch-2 sp, ch 2**, 2 dc in next ch-2 sp, rep from * twice, rep from * to ** once, join with a Sl st in 3rd ch of beg ch-3. Fasten off C.

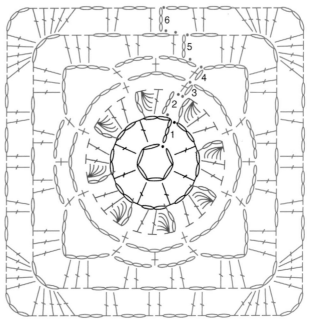

33 | VENETIAN STAR

SKILL LEVEL: Intermediate

Beginning popcorn (beg pc): Ch 3 (counts as dc), 4 dc in same st or sp, drop loop from hook, insert hook in the 3rd ch of beg ch-3, pick up the dropped loop and draw through.

Popcorn (pc): Work 5 dc in same st or sp, drop loop from hook, insert hook in the first of the 5 dc just made, pick up dropped loop and draw through.

Ch 4, join with a Sl st to form a ring.

RND 1: Ch 3 (counts as dc here and throughout), 11 dc in ring, join with a Sl st in 3rd ch of beg ch-3 (12 dc).

RND 2: Beg pc in first st, (ch 1, pc) in each of next 2 dc, *ch 5, (1 pc, ch 1) in each of next 2 dc, 1 pc in next dc, rep from * twice, ch 5, join with a Sl st in 3rd ch of beg ch-3.

RND 3: Sl st in next ch-1 sp, beg pc in first sp, ch 1, 1 pc in next ch-1 sp, *ch 2, 5 dc in next ch-5 sp, ch 2**, 1 pc in next ch-1 sp, ch 1, 1 pc in next ch-1 sp, rep from * twice, rep from * to ** once, join with a Sl st in 3rd ch of beg ch-3.

RND 4: Sl st in next ch-1 sp, beg pc in first sp, *ch 3, sk next ch-2 sp, (1 dc, ch 1) in each of next 2 dc, (1 dc, ch 1, 1 dc, ch 1, 1 dc) in next dc, (ch 1, 1 dc) in each of next 2 dc, ch 3, sk next ch-2 sp**, 1 pc in next ch-1 sp, rep from * twice, rep from * to ** once, join with a Sl st in 3rd ch of beg ch-3.

RND 5: Ch 3, *3 dc in next ch-3 sp, [1 dc in next dc, 1 dc in next ch-1 sp] 3 times, (2 dc, ch 3, 2 dc) in next dc (corner), [1 dc in next ch-1 sp, 1 dc in next dc] 3 times, 3 dc in next ch-3 sp**, dc in next pc, rep from * twice, rep from * to ** once, join with Sl st in 3rd ch of beg ch-3.

RND 6: Ch 1, starting in same st, 1 sc in each of next 12 dc, *(2 sc, ch 2, 2 sc) in next ch-3 sp (corner)**, 1 sc in each of next 23 dc, rep from * twice, rep from * to ** once, 1 sc in each of next 11 dc, join with a Sl st in first sc. Fasten off.

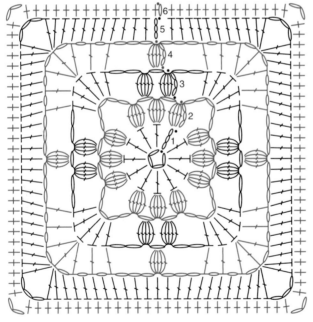

34 | FLOWER GARDEN SQUARE I

SKILL LEVEL: Intermediate

Made with 3 colors: A, B, and C.

With A, ch 6, join with a Sl st to form a ring.

RND 1: With A, work 20 sc in ring, join with a Sl st in first sc (20 sc).

RND 2: With A, ch 1, working through front loops of sts, 1 sc in first sc, *1 hdc in the next sc, 3 dc in next sc, 1 hdc in next sc**, 1 sc in next sc, rep from * 3 times, rep from * to ** once, join with a Sl st in first sc (5 petals). Fasten off A.

RND 3: With right side facing, working in the remaining back loops of sts in rnd 1, join B in next sc, *ch 8, sk next 4 sts, Sl st in next sc, rep from * 3 times more (4 ch-8 sps).

RND 4: With B, ch 1, 16 sc in each ch-8 sp around, join with a Sl st in first sc (64 sc).

RND 5: With B, Sl st in next 3 sc, ch 4 (counts as 1 dc, ch 1), (1 dc, ch 1) in each of next 9 sc, sk next 6 sc, *(1 dc, ch 1) in the next 10 sc, sk next 6 sc, rep from * twice, join with Sl st in 3rd ch of beg ch-4. Fasten off B.

RND 6: With right side facing, join C in last ch-1 sp made, ch 1, sc in first sp, *ch 6, sk next 2 dc**, 1 sc in next ch-1 sp, rep from * 18 times, rep from * to ** once, join with a Sl st in first sc (20 ch-6 sps).

RND 7: With C, Sl st in first 2 ch sts of next ch-6 sp, ch 1, 1 sc in same sp, *(ch 6, 1 sc) in each of next 4 next ch-6 sps**, 1 sc in next ch-6 sp, rep from * twice, rep from * to ** once, join with a Sl st in first sc (16 ch-6 sps).

RND 8: With C, ch 1, sc in first sc, *4 sc in next ch-6 sp, 1 sc in next sc, 4 sc in next ch-6 sp, (1 dc ch 3, 1 dc) in next sc (corner), [4 sc in next ch-6 sp, 1 sc in next sc] twice**, sc in each of next 2 sc, rep from * twice, rep from * to ** once, sc in next sc, join with a Sl st in first sc. Fasten off C.

35 | FLOWER GARDEN SQUARE II

SKILL LEVEL: Intermediate

Made with 2 colors: A and B.

With A, ch 6, join with a Sl st to form a ring.

RND 1: With A, work 20 sc in ring, join with a Sl st in first sc (20 sc).

RND 2: With A, ch 1, working in front loops of sts, 1 sc in same st, *1 hdc in the next sc, (1 tr, 1 picot, 1 tr) in next sc, 1 hdc in next sc**, 1 sc in next sc, rep from * 3 times, rep from * to ** once, join with a Sl st in first sc (5 petals). Fasten off A.

RND 3: With right side facing, working in remaining back loops of sts in rnd 1, join B in next sc, *ch 8, sk next 4 sts, Sl st in next sc, rep from * 3 times (4 ch-8 sps).

RND 4: With B, ch 1, work 16 sc in each ch-8 sp around, join with a Sl st in first sc (64 sc).

RND 5: With B, Sl st in next 3 sc, ch 4 (counts as 1 dc, ch 1), (1 dc, ch 1) in each of next 9 sc, sk next 6 sts, *(1 dc, ch 1) in each of next 10 sc, sk next 6 sc, rep from * twice, join with a Sl st in 3rd ch of beg ch-4. Fasten off B.

RND 6: With right side facing, join A in last ch-1 sp made, ch 1, sc in first st, *ch 6, sk next ch-1 sp**, 1 sc in next ch-1 sp, rep from * 18 times, rep from * to ** once, join with a Sl st in first sc (20 ch-6 sps).

RND 7: With A, Sl st in next 2 ch sts of next ch-6 sp, ch 1, 1 sc in same sp, *(ch 6, 1 sc) in each of next 4 next ch-6 sps**, 1 sc in next ch-6 sp, rep from * twice, rep from * to ** once, join with a Sl st in first sc (16 ch-6 sps).

RND 8: With A, ch 1, sc in first sc, *4 sc in next ch-6 sp, 1 sc in next sc, 4 sc in next ch-6 sp, (1 dc ch 3, 1 dc) in next sc (corner), [4 sc in next ch-6 sp, 1 sc in next sc] twice**, sc in each of next 2 sc, rep from * twice, rep from * to ** once, sc in next sc, join with a Sl st in first sc. Fasten off A.

36 | FLOWER GARDEN SQUARE III

SKILL LEVEL: Intermediate

Made with 3 colors: A, B, and C.

With A, ch 6, join with a Sl st to form a ring.

RND 1: With A, work 20 sc in ring, join with a Sl st in first sc (20 sc).

RND 2: With A, ch 1, working through front loops of sts, sc in first sc, *ch 4, sk next 4 sc, 1 sc in next sc, rep from * 3 times, ch 4, join with a Sl st in first sc (5 ch-4 sps).

RND 3: With A, ch 3 (counts as dc), (5 dc, ch 3, 6 dc) in next ch-4 sp, (6 dc, ch 3, 6 dc) in each ch-4 sp around, join with a Sl st in 3rd ch of beg ch-3. Fasten off A.

RND 4: With right side facing, working in back loops of sts in rnd 1, join B in next sc, *ch 8, sk next 4 sts, Sl st in next sc, rep from * 3 times (4 ch-8 sps).

RND 5: With B, ch 1, 16 sc in each ch-8 sp around, join with a Sl st to first sc (64 sc).

RND 6: With B, Sl st in next 3 sc, ch 4 (counts as 1 dc, ch 1), (1 dc, ch 1) in each of next 9 sc, sk next 6 sc, *(1 dc, ch 1) in each of next 10 sc, sk next 6 sc, rep from * twice, join with a Sl st in 3rd ch of beg ch-4. Fasten off B.

RND 7: With right side facing, join C in last ch-1 sp made, ch 1, 1 sc in same sp, *ch 6, sk next 2 dc**, 1 sc in next ch-1 sp, rep from * 18 times, rep from * to ** once, join with a Sl st in first sc (20 ch-6 sps).

RND 8: With C, Sl st in first 2 ch sts of next ch-6 sp, ch 1, 1 sc in same sp, *(ch 6, 1 sc) in each of next 4 ch-6 sps**, 1 sc in next ch-6 sp, rep from * twice, rep from * to ** once, join with a Sl st in first sc (16 ch-6 sps).

RND 9: With C, ch 1, sc in first sc, *4 sc in next ch-6 sp, 1 sc in next sc, 4 sc in next ch-6 sp, (1 dc, ch 3, 1 dc) in next sc (corner), [4 sc in next ch-6 sp, 1 sc in next sc] twice**, sc in each of next 2 sc, rep from * twice, rep from * to ** once, sc in next sc, join with a Sl st in first sc. Fasten off C.

37 | FLOWER GARDEN SQUARE IV

SKILL LEVEL: Intermediate

Made with 3 colors: A, B, and C.

Puff stitch (puff st): [Yo, insert hook in next st, yo, draw yarn through st] 4 times in same st, yo, draw yarn through 9 loops on hook.

With A, ch 6, join with a Sl st to form a ring.

RND 1: With A, work 20 sc in ring, join with a Sl st in first sc (20 sc).

RND 2: With A, working through front loops of sts, *ch 8, sk next sc, puff st in next sc, ch 8, sk next sc, Sl st next st, rep from * 4 times, ending with last Sl st in first Sl st (5 petals).

RND 3: With A, ch 1, work 12 sc in each ch-8 sp around, join with a Sl st in first sc. Fasten off A.

RND 4: With right side facing, working in back loops of sts in rnd 1, join B in next sc, *ch 8, sk next 4 sts, Sl st in next sc, rep from * 3 times (4 ch-8 sps).

RND 5: With B, ch 1, work 16 sc in each ch-8 sp around, join with a Sl st in first sc (64 sc).

RND 6: With B, Sl st in next 3 sc, ch 4 (counts as 1 dc, ch 1), (1 dc, ch 1) in each of next 9 sc, sk next 6 sc, *(1 dc, ch 1) in each of next 10 sc, sk next 6 sc, rep from * twice, join with a Sl st in 3rd ch of beg ch-4. Fasten off B.

RND 7: With right side facing, join C in last ch-1 sp made, ch 1, 1 sc in same sp, *ch 6, sk next ch-1 sp**, 1 sc in next ch-1 sp, rep from * 18 times, rep from * to ** once, join with a Sl st in first sc (20 ch-6 sps).

RND 8: With C, Sl st in first 2 chs sts of next ch-6 sp, ch 1, 1 sc in same sp, *(ch 6, 1 sc) in each of next 4 next ch-6 sps**, 1 sc in next ch-6 sp, rep from * twice, rep from * to ** once, join with a Sl st in first sc (16 ch-6 sps).

RND 9: With C, ch 1, sc in first sc, *4 sc in next ch-6 sp, 1 sc in next sc, 4 sc in next ch-6 sp, (1 dc ch 3, 1 dc) in next sc (corner), [4 sc in next ch-6 sp, 1 sc in next sc] twice**, sc in each of next 2 sc, rep from * twice, rep from * to ** once, sc in next sc, join with a Sl st in first sc. Fasten off C.

38 | FLOWER GARDEN SQUARE V

SKILL LEVEL: Intermediate

Made with 2 colors: A and B.

With A, ch 6, join with a Sl st to form a ring.

RND 1: With A, work 20 sc in ring, join with a Sl st in first sc (20 sc).

RND 2: With A, working through front loops of sts, (1 sc, ch 12) in each sc around, join with Sl st in first sc (20 ch-12 sps). Fasten off A.

RND 3: With right side facing, working in back loops of sts in rnd 1, join B in next sc, *ch 8, sk next 4 sc, Sl st in next sc, rep from * 3 times, ending with last Sl st in first Sl st (4 ch-8 sps).

RND 4: With B, work 16 sc in each ch-8 sp around, join with a Sl st in first sc (64 sc).

RND 5: With B, Sl st in next 3 sc, ch 4 (counts as 1 dc, ch 1), (1 dc, ch 1) in each of next 9 sc, sk next 6 sc, *(1 dc, ch 1) in each of next 10 sc, sk next 6 sc, rep from * 3 times, join with a Sl st in 3rd ch of beg ch-4. Fasten off B.

RND 6: With right side facing, join A in last ch-1 sp made, *ch 6, sk next ch-1 sp**, 1 sc in next ch-1 sp, rep from * 18 times, rep from * to ** once, join with a Sl st in first sc (20 ch-6 sps).

RND 7: With A, Sl st in first 2 ch sts of next ch-6 sp, ch 1, 1 sc in same sp, *(ch 6, 1 sc) in each of next 4 next ch-6 sps**, 1 sc in next ch-6 sp, rep from * twice, rep from * to ** once, join with a Sl st in first sc (16 ch-6 sps).

RND 8: With A, ch 1, sc in first sc, *4 sc in next ch-6 sp, 1 sc in next sc, 4 sc in next ch-6 sp, (1 dc ch 3, 1 dc) in next sc (corner), [4 sc in next ch-6 sp, 1 sc in next sc] twice**, sc in each of next 2 sc, rep from * twice, rep from * to ** once, sc in next sc, join with a Sl st in first sc. Fasten off A.

39 | FLOWER GARDEN SQUARE VI

SKILL LEVEL: Intermediate

Made with 3 colors: A, B, and C.

Long single crochet (Lsc): Insert hook in designated st 2 rnds below, draw loop up to current level of work, yo, draw yarn through 2 loops on hook.

With A, ch 6, join with a Sl st to form a ring.

RND 1: With A, work 20 sc in ring, join with a Sl st in first sc (20 sc).

RND 2: With A, ch 1, working through the front loops of sts, 1 sc in first sc, *ch 3, sk next 3 sc, 1 sc in the next sc, rep from * 3 times, ch 3, join with a Sl st in first sc (5 ch-3 sps).

RND 3: With A, ch 1, (1 sc, 1 hdc, 3 dc, 1 hdc, 1 sc) in each ch-3 sp around, join with a Sl st in first sc. Fasten off A.

RND 4: With right side facing, join B in first sc, ch 1, starting in same st, *1 sc in sc, 2 hdc in next hdc, 2 dc in each of next 3 dc, 2 hdc in next hdc, 1 sc in next sc, working over sts in rnd 3, work 1 Lsc in next sc between petals in rnd 2, rep from * around, join with a Sl st in first sc. Fasten off B.

RND 5: With right side facing, working in back loops of sts in rnd 1, join C in next sc, ch 1, 1 sc in same st, *ch 8, sk next 4 sc**, 1 sc in next st, rep from * 3 times, rep from * to ** once, join with a Sl st in first sc (4 ch-8 sps).

RND 6: With C, ch 1, work 16 sc in each ch-8 sp around, join with a Sl st in first sc (64 sc).

RND 7: With C, Sl st in next 3 sc, ch 4 (counts as 1 dc, ch 1), (1 dc, ch 1) in each of next 9 sc, sk next 6 sc, *(1 dc, ch 1) in each of next 10 sc, sk next 6 sc, rep from * twice, join with a Sl st in 3rd ch of beg ch-4. Fasten off C.

RND 8: With right side facing, join A in last ch-1 sp made, ch 1, 1 sc in same ch-1 sp, *ch 6, sk next ch-1 sp**, 1 sc in next ch-1 sp, rep from * 18 times, rep from * to ** once, join with a Sl st in first sc (20 ch-6 sps).

RND 9: With A, Sl st in first 2 ch sts of next ch-6 sp, ch 1, 1 sc in same sp, *(ch 6, 1 sc) in each of next 4 next ch-6 sps**, 1 sc in next ch-6 sp, rep from * twice, rep from * to ** once, join with a Sl st in first sc (16 ch-6 sps).

RND 10: With A, ch 1, sc in first sc, *4 sc in next ch-6 sp, 1 sc in next sc, 4 sc in next ch-6 sp, (1 dc ch 3, 1 dc) in next sc (corner), [4 sc in next ch-6 sp 1 sc in next sc] twice**, sc in each of next 2 sc, rep from * twice, rep from * to ** once, sc in next sc, join with a Sl st in first sc. Fasten off A.

40 | FLOWER GARDEN SQUARE VII

SKILL LEVEL: Intermediate

Made with 3 colors: A, B, and C.

Bullion stitch: Yo (10 times), pick up a loop in designated stitch, yo, draw through all loops on hook, ch 1 to lock st.

With A, ch 6, join with a Sl st to form a ring.

RND 1: With A, Work 20 sc in ring, join with a Sl st in first sc (20 sc).

RND 2: With A, ch 1, working through front loops of sts, starting in same st, *1 sc in sc, 1 hdc in next sc, 3 bullion sts in next sc, 1 hdc in next sc, rep from * around, join with a Sl st in first sc (5 bullion petals). Fasten off A.

RND 3: Join B in any back lp of 2nd 2. With B, ch 1, working in back loops of sts in rnd 2, *ch 8, sk next 4 sts, Sl st in next st, rep from * 3 times, ending with last Sl st in first Sl st (4 ch-8 sps).

RND 4: With B, ch 1, work 16 sc in each ch-8 sp around, join with a Sl st in first sc.

RND 5: With B, Sl st in next 3 sc, ch 4 (counts as dc, ch 1), (1 dc, ch 1) in each of next 9 sc, sk next 6 sc, *(1 dc, ch 1) in each of next 10 sc, sk next 6 sc, rep from * twice, join with a Sl st in 3rd ch of beg ch-4. Fasten off B.

RND 6: With right side facing, join C in last ch-1 sp made, ch 1, sc in first st, *ch 6, sk next ch-1 sp**, 1 sc in next ch-1 sp, rep from * 18 times, rep from * to ** once, join with a Sl st in first sc (20 ch-6 sps).

RND 7: With C, Sl st in first 2 ch sts of next ch-6 sp, ch 1, 1 sc in same sp, *(ch 6, 1 sc) in each of next 4 ch-6 sps**, 1 sc in next ch-6 sp, rep from * twice, rep from * to ** once, join with a Sl st in first sc (16 ch-6 sps).

RND 8: With C, ch 1, sc in first sc, *4 sc in next ch-6 sp, 1 sc in next sc, 4 sc in next ch-6 sp, (1 dc ch 3, 1 dc) in next sc (corner), [4 sc in next ch-6 sp 1 sc in next sc] twice**, sc in each of next 2 sc, rep from * twice, rep from * to ** once, sc in next sc, join with a Sl st in first sc. Fasten off C.

41 | FLOWER GARDEN SQUARE VIII

SKILL LEVEL: Intermediate

Made with 3 colors: A, B, and C.

Picot: Ch 3, Sl st in 3rd ch from hook.

With A, ch 6, join with a Sl st to form a ring.

RND 1: With A, ch 1, work 20 sc in ring, join with a Sl st in first sc (20 sc). Fasten off A.

RND 2: With right side facing, working in front loops of sts, join B in any sc, ch 4 (counts as tr), 1 sc in next sc *1 tr in next sc, 1 sc in next sc, rep from * 9 times, join with a Sl st to 3rd ch of beg ch-3 (10 tr, 10 sc). Fasten off B.

RND 3: With right side facing, join C in any sc, ch 1, sc in same st, *ch 3, sk next tr, 1 sc in next sc, rep from * 8 times, ch 3, join with a Sl st in first sc (10 ch-3 sps).

RND 4: With C, ch 1, (1 sc, 1 hdc, 1 dc, picot, 1 dc, 1 hdc, 1 sc) in each ch-3 sp around (10 shells). Fasten off C.

RND 5: With right side facing, working in remaining back loops of sts in rnd 1, join A in next sc, ch 1, 1 sc in same st, *ch 8, sk next 4 sts, 1 sc in next sc, rep from * twice, ch 8, join with a Sl st in first sc (4 ch-8 sps).

RND 6: With A, ch 1, work 16 sc in each ch-8 sp around, join with a Sl st in first sc (64 sc).

RND 7: With A, Sl st in next 3 sc, ch 4 (counts as 1 dc, ch 1), (1 dc, ch 1) in each of next 9 sc, sk next 6 sts, *(1 dc, ch 1) in each of next 10 sc, sk next 6 sc, rep from * twice, join with a Sl st in 3rd ch of beg ch-4. Fasten off A.

RND 8: With right side facing, join B in last ch-1 sp made, ch 1, sc in same ch-1 sp, *ch 6, sk next ch-1 sp**, 1 sc in next ch-1 sp, rep from * 18 times, rep from * to ** once, join with a Sl st in first sc (20 ch-6 sps).

RND 9: With B, Sl st in next 2 ch sts of next ch-6 sp, ch 1, 1 sc in same sp, *(ch 6, 1 sc) in each of next 4 ch-6 sps**, 1 sc in next ch-6 sp, rep from * twice, rep from * to ** once, join with a Sl st in first sc (16 ch-6 sps).

RND 10: With B, ch 1, sc in first sc, *4 sc in next ch-6 sp, 1 sc in next sc, 4 sc in next ch-6 sp, (1 dc, ch 3, 1 dc) in next sc (corner), [4 sc in next ch-6 sp, 1 sc in next sc] twice**, sc in each of next 2 sc, rep from * twice, rep from * to ** once, sc in next sc, join with a Sl st in first sc. Fasten off B.

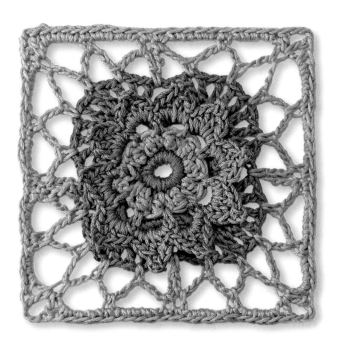

42 | FLOWER GARDEN SQUARE IX

SKILL LEVEL: Intermediate

Made with 4 colors: A, B, C, and D.

In round 5, you will be working 2 rounds below in the free loops of round 3.

With A, ch 4, join with a Sl st to form a ring.

RND 1: With A, ch 1, work 8 sc in ring, join with a Sl st in first sc (8 sc).

RND 2: With A, ch 1, 2 sc in each sc around (16 sc), turn.

RND 3: With wrong side facing and A, working in the back loops only, *1 tr in next st, 1 Sl st in next st, rep from * 7 times, join with a Sl st in first sc (98 tr, 8 sc), turn.

RND 4: With right side facing and A, working back loops of sts in rnd 3, *ch 2, 3 tr in next st, ch 2, Sl st in next st, rep from * 7 times, ending with last Sl st in first Sl st (8 petals). Fasten off A.

RND 5: With right side facing, working in Sl sts between petals in rnd 3, join B in first Sl st, ch 1, sc in same Sl st, *ch 5, sk next petal, 1 sc in next Sl st, rep from * 6 times, ch 3, hdc in first sc instead of last ch-5 sp (8 ch-5 sps).

RND 6: With B, ch 3 (counts as dc here and throughout), 2 dc in same sp (half corner), *ch 2, 3 dc in next ch-5 sp, ch 2**, (3 dc, ch 3, 3 dc) in next ch-5 sp (corner made), rep from * twice, rep from * to ** once, 3 dc in same sp as half corner, ch 3, join with a Sl st in 3rd ch of beg ch-3 (completes corner). Fasten off B.

RND 7: With right side facing, join C in any ch-3 corner sp, ch 1, 3 sc in same sp (half corner made), *(ch 2, 3 sc) in each of next 2 ch-2 sps, ch 2**, (3 sc, ch 3, 3 sc) in next ch-3 sp (corner made), rep from * twice, rep from * to ** once, 3 sc in same sp as first half corner, ch 3, join with a Sl st in 3rd ch of beg ch-3 (completes corner). Fasten off C.

RND 8: With right side facing, join D in any corner ch-3 sp, ch 3, 2 dc in same sp (half corner) *[ch 2, 3 dc in next ch-2 sp] 3 times, ch 2**, (3 dc, ch 3, 3 dc) in next ch-3 sp (corner), rep from * twice, rep from * to ** once, 3 dc same sp as first half corner, ch 3, join with a Sl st in 3rd ch of beg ch-3 (completes corner). Fasten off D.

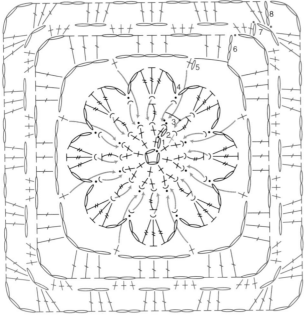

43 | FLOWER GARDEN SQUARE X

SKILL LEVEL: Intermediate

Made with 3 colors: A, B, and C.

Double crochet 2 together (dc2tog): [Yo, insert hook in next st, yo, draw yarn through, yo, draw through 2 loops on hook] twice, yo, draw through 3 loops on hook.

With A, ch 4, join with a Sl st to form a ring.

RND 1: With A, ch 3 (counts as dc here and throughout), 15 dc in ring, join with a Sl st to 3rd ch of beg ch-3 (16 dc).

RND 2: With A, ch 3, 1 dc in same st, 2 dc in each dc around, join with a Sl st in 3rd ch of beg ch-3 (32 dc). Fasten off A.

RND 3: With right side facing, working in front loops only of sts, join B in first st, *sc in next st, ch 3, dc2tog worked across next 2 dc, ch 3, Sl st in next dc, rep from * around, join with a Sl st in first Sl st (8 petals).

RND 4: With B, Sl st in next sc, ch 1, *4 sc in next ch-3 sp, (1 sc, ch 3, 1 sc) in next dc2tog, 4 sc in next ch-3 sp, rep from * around, join with a Sl st in first sc. Drop B to wrong side.

RND 5: With right side facing, working in remaining back loops of sts in rnd 2, join C in first dc in rnd 2, ch 3 (half corner made), *1 dc in each of next 7 dc**, (1 dc, ch 3, 1 dc) in next dc (corner), rep from * twice, rep * to ** once, 1 dc in same st as beg ch-3, ch 1, hdc in 3rd ch of beg ch-3 (completes corner).

RND 6: With C, ch 3, 2 dc in same sp (half corner made), *1 dc in each of next 9 dc**, [3 dc, ch 3, 3 dc] in next ch-3 sp (corner), rep from * twice, rep from * to ** once, join with a Sl st in 3rd ch of beg ch-3 (completes corner). Drop C to wrong side. Pick up B and draw through loop on hook.

RND 7: With B, ch 1, starting in same st, *sc in each of next 15 dc**, (2 sc, ch 2, 2 sc) in next ch-3 sp, rep from * twice, rep from * to ** once, join with a Sl st in first sc. Fasten off B. Pick up C and draw through loop on hook.

RND 8: With C, ch 1, starting in same st, 1 sc in each of next 17 sc, *(2 sc, ch 2, 2 sc) in next ch-2 sp (corner made)**, 1 sc in each of next 19 sc, rep from * twice, rep from * to ** once, 1 sc in each of next 2 sc, join with a Sl st in first sc. Fasten off C.

44 | FLOWER GARDEN SQUARE XI

SKILL LEVEL: Intermediate

Made with 3 colors: A, B, and C.

With A, ch 4, join with a Sl st to form a ring.

RND 1: With A, ch 4 (counts as dc, ch 1), [1 dc, ch 1] 7 times in ring, join with a Sl st in 3rd ch of beg ch-4 (8 ch-1 sps). Fasten off A.

RND 2: With right side facing, join B in any ch-1 sp, ch 2 (counts as hdc), (1 dc, 1 tr, 1 dc, 1 hdc) in same sp, (1 hdc, 1 dc, 1 tr, 1 dc, 1 hdc) in each ch-1 sp around, join with a Sl st in 2nd ch of beg ch-2 (8 petals).

RND 3: With B, ch 1, *2 sc in each of next 4 sts, Sl st next st, rep from * around, join with a Sl st in first sc. Fasten off B.

RND 4: With right side facing, working behind sts in rnd 3, join A in any dc between petals in rnd 1, ch 1, sc in same st, *ch 5, sk next petal, sc in next dc in rnd 1, rep from * 6 times, ch 5, join with a Sl st in first sc (8 ch-5 sps).

RND 5: With A, Sl st in next ch-5 sp, ch 3 (counts as dc here and throughout), (2 dc, ch 3, 3 dc) in same sp (half corner), *ch 2, 1 sc in 3rd ch of next ch-5 sp, ch 2**, (3 dc, ch 2, 3 dc) in next ch-5 sp (corner), rep from * twice, rep from * to ** once, join with a Sl st in 3rd ch of beg ch-3. Fasten off A.

RND 6: With right side facing, join C in any ch-3 corner sp, ch 3, (2 dc, ch 3, 3 dc) in same corner, *(ch 2, 2 dc) in each of next 2 ch-2 sps, ch 2**, (3 dc, ch 3, 3 dc) in next ch-2 sp (corner), rep from * twice, rep from * to ** once, join with a Sl st in 3rd ch of beg ch-3.

RND 7: With C, Sl st in next 2 dc and in next ch-3 sp, ch 3, (2 dc, ch 3, 3 dc) in same sp, *(ch 2, 2 dc) in each of next 3 ch-2 sps, ch 2**, (3 dc, ch 3, 3 dc) in next ch-3 sp (corner), rep from * twice, rep from * to ** once, join with a Sl st in 3rd ch of beg ch-3.

RND 8: With C, ch 1, 1 sc in each dc, 2 sc in each ch-2 sp, (2 sc, ch 3, 2 sc) in each corner ch-3 sp, join with a Sl st in first sc. Fasten off C.

45 | FLOWER GARDEN SQUARE XII

SKILL LEVEL: Intermediate

Made with 4 colors: A, B, C, and D.

Puff stitch (puff st): [Yo, insert hook in next st, yo, draw yarn through st] 4 times in same st, yo, draw yarn through 9 loops on hook.

Beg cluster: Ch 3, [yo, insert hook in st or sp, yo, draw up a loop, yo, draw through 2 lps] twice in same st or sp, yo, draw through 3 loops on hook.

Cluster: [Yo, insert hook in st or sp, yo, draw up a loop, yo, draw through 2 loops on hook] 3 times in same st or sp, yo, draw through 4 loops on hook.

With A, ch 5, join with a Sl st to form a ring.

RND 1: With A, ch 4 (counts as 1 dc, ch-1), [1 dc, ch 1] 15 times in ring, join with a Sl st in 3rd ch of beg ch-4 (16 ch-1 sps). Fasten off A.

RND 2: With right side facing, join B in any ch-1 sp, ch 3, (puff st, ch 1) in each ch-1 sp around, join with a Sl st in 3rd ch of beg ch-3. Fasten off B.

RND 3: With right side facing, join C in any ch-1 sp, beg cluster in same sp, *(ch 1, cluster) in each of next 3 ch-1 sps, ch 3**, cluster in next ch-1 sp, rep from * twice, rep from * to ** once (16 clusters). Fasten off C.

RND 4: With right side facing, join D in any ch-3 sp, ch 3, work 2 dc in same sp (half corner made), *3 dc in each of next 3 ch-1 sps**, (3 dc, ch 3, 3 dc) in next ch-3 sp (corner made), rep from * twice, rep from * to ** once, 3 dc in same sp as beg half corner, ch 3, join with a Sl st in 3rd ch of beg ch-3 (completes corner). Fasten off D.

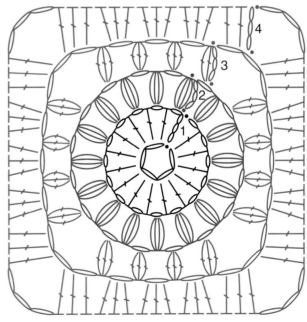

46 | PICOT ROSE

SKILL LEVEL: Intermediate

Made with 3 colors: A, B, and C.

Picot: Ch 4, Sl st in 4th ch from hook.

With A, ch 4, join with a Sl st to form a ring.

RND 1: With A, ch 5 (counts as a dc, ch 2), [1 dc, ch 2] 7 times in ring, join with a Sl st in 3rd ch of beg ch-5 (8 ch-2 sps, 8 dc). Fasten off A.

RND 2: With right side facing, join B in any ch-2 sp, ch 4 (counts as dc, ch 1), [picot, ch 1] twice, *1 dc in next ch-2 sp, [ch 1, picot] twice, ch 1, rep from * around, join with a Sl st in 3rd ch of the beg ch-4. Fasten off B.

RND 3: With right side facing, join C in any ch-1 sp between 2 picots, ch 1, 1 sc in same sp, *ch 7, sk 2 picots**, 1 sc in next ch-1 sp between 2 picots, rep from * 5 times, rep from * to ** once, join with a Sl st in first sc.

RND 4: With C, Sl st in next ch-7 sp, ch 1, [1 sc, 1 hdc, 9 dc, 1 hdc, 1 sc] in each ch-7 sp around, join with a Sl st in first sc. Fasten off C.

RND 5: With right side facing, join B in any sp between 2 sc in rnd 4, ch 4 (counts as tr), 1 tr in same sp (half corner made), *ch 3, sk next 4 sts, 1 sc in each of next 5 dc, sk next 8 sts, 1 sc in each of next 5 dc, ch 3, sk next 4 sts**, (2 tr, ch 3, 2 tr) in sp between last skipped and next sc (corner made), rep from * twice, rep from * to ** once, 2 tr in same sp as first half corner, ch 3, join with a Sl st in 3rd ch of beg ch-3 (completes corner).

RND 6: With B, ch 1, 1 sc in first 2 tr, *[3 sc in next ch-3 sp, 1 sc in each of next 5 sc] twice, 3 sc in next ch-3 sp, sc in each of next 2 tr, (2 sc, ch 3, 2 sc) in next ch-3 sp**, 1 sc in each of next 2 tr, rep from * twice, rep from * to ** once, join with a Sl st in first sc. Fasten off.

47 | CELTIC CROSS

SKILL LEVEL: Intermediate

Ch 6, join with a Sl st to form a ring.

RND 1: Ch 3, (counts as dc here and throughout), work 15 dc into ring, join with a Sl st in 3rd ch of beg ch-3 (16 dc).

RND 2: Ch 3, 2 dc in same st, *ch 2, sk next dc, 1 dc in next dc, ch 2, sk next dc**, 3 dc in next dc, rep from * twice, rep from * to ** once, join with a Sl st in 3rd ch of beg ch-3.

RND 3: Ch 3, *5 dc in next dc, 1 dc in next dc**, [ch 2, 1 dc in next dc] twice, rep from * twice, rep from * to ** once, join with a Sl st in 3rd ch of beg ch-3.

RND 4: Ch 3, 1 dc in each of next 2 dc, *5 dc in next dc, 1 dc in each of next 3 dc, ch 2, 1 dc in next dc, ch 2**, 1 dc in each of next 3 dc, rep from * twice, rep from * to ** once, join with a Sl st in 3rd ch of beg ch-3.

RND 5: Ch 3, 1 dc in each of next 4 dc, *5 dc in next dc, 1 dc in each of next 5 dc, ch 2, 1 dc in next dc, ch 2**, 1 dc in each of next 5 dc, rep from * twice, rep from * to ** once, join with a Sl st in 3rd ch of beg ch-3.

RND 6: Ch 4 (counts as dc, ch 1), [sk next dc, 1 dc in next dc, ch 1] 3 times, *(1 dc, ch 2, 1 dc) in next st (corner) *ch 1, 1 dc in next dc [ch 1, sk next dc, 1 dc in next dc] 3 times**, [ch 2, 1 dc in next dc] twice, [ch 1, sk next dc, 1 dc in next dc] 3 times, rep from * twice, rep from * to ** once, ch 2, 1 dc in next dc, ch 2, join with a Sl st in 3rd ch of beg ch-4.

RND 7: Ch 3, 1 dc in next ch-1 sp, 2 dc in each of next 3 ch-1 sps, *(3 dc, ch 2, 3 dc) in next ch-2 sp (corner made), 2 dc in each of next 4 ch-1 sps, 3 dc in each of next 2 ch-2 sps**, 2 dc in each of next 4 ch-1 sps, rep from * twice, rep from * to ** once, join with a Sl st in 3rd ch of beg ch-3.

RND 8: Ch 1, starting in same st, 1 sc in each of first 11 dc, *(1 sc, ch 2, 1 sc) in next ch-2 sp (corner made), 1 sc in each of the next 28 dc, rep from * twice, 1 sc in each of next 17 dc, join with a Sl st in first sc. Fasten off.

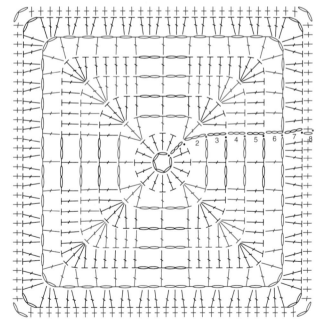

48 | ROSE OF SHARON

SKILL LEVEL: Intermediate

Made with 3 colors: A, B, and C.

Beginning popcorn (beg pc): Ch 3 (counts as dc), 4 dc in same st or sp, drop lp from hook, insert hook in the 3rd ch of beg ch-3, pick up the dropped lp and draw through.

Popcorn (pc): Work 5 dc in same st or sp, drop lp from hook, insert hook in the first of the 5 dc just made, pick up dropped lp and draw through.

Long double crochet (long dc): Yo, insert hook in designated st, yo, draw yarn through sts and draw up to current level of work, [yo, draw yarn through 2 lps on hook] twice.

Long triple crochet (long tr): Yo (twice), insert hook in designated st, yo, draw yarn through sts and draw up to current level of work, [yo, draw yarn through 2 lps on hook] 3 times.

Ch 4, join with a Sl st to form a ring.

RND 1: Ch 3 (counts as dc here and throughout), work 11 dc in ring, join with a Sl st in 3rd ch of beg ch-3 (12 dc).

RND 2: Beg pc in first st, ch 2, (pc, ch 2) in the each dc around, join in 3rd ch of beg ch-3 (12 pc). Drop A to wrong side.

RND 3: With RS facing, join B in first pc, ch 1, sc in first st, *1 sc in the next ch-2 sp, 1 long dc in base of next pc, 1 sc in same ch-2 sp, 1 sc in next pc, rep from * around, omitting last sc, join with a Sl st in first sc.

RND 4: Ch 1, 1 sc in back loop of each st around, join with a Sl st in the first sc. Drop B to wrong side, pick up loop of A.

RND 5: With A, beg pc in first sc, ch 3, sk next 2 sc, *pc in next dc, ch 3, sk next 2 sc, rep from * around, join with a Sl st in beg pc (16 pc). Fasten off A, pick up loop of B.

RND 6: With B, ch 1, 1 sc in first st, *1 sc in next ch-3 sp, 1 long tr in each of next 2 sc 2 rnds below, 1 sc in the same ch-3 sp, 1 sc in next pc, rep from * around, omitting last sc, join with a Sl st in first sc. Fasten off B.

RND 7: With RS facing, join C between any 2 long tr, ch 3, 2 dc in same sp (half corner made), *[ch 2, sk next 3 sc, 2 dc in sp between next 2 long tr] 3 times, ch 2, sk next 3 sc**, (3 dc, ch 3, 3 dc) in sp between next 2 long tr (corner made), rep from * twice, rep from * to ** once, 3 dc in same sp as first half corner, ch 3, join with a Sl st in 3rd ch of beg ch-3 (corner completed).

RND 8: With C, ch 1, starting in same st, *1 sc in each of next 3 dc, [2 sc in next ch-2 sp, 1 sc in each of next 2 dc] 3 times, 2 sc in next ch-2 sp, (1 sc, ch 3, 1 sc) in next ch-3 sp (corner), rep from * 3 times, join with a Sl st in first sc. Fasten off C.

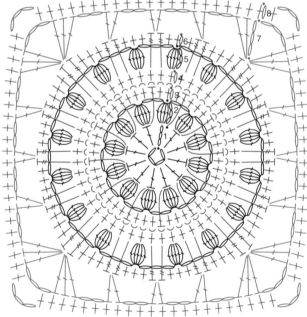

49 | WILD FLOWER

SKILL LEVEL: Intermediate

Made with 3 colors: A, B, and C.

Beginning popcorn (beg pc): Ch 3 (counts as dc), 4 dc in same st or sp, drop lp from hook, insert hook in the 3rd ch of beg ch-3, pick up the dropped lp and draw through.

Popcorn: Work 5 dc in same st or sp, drop lp from hook, insert hook in the first of the 5 dc just made, pick up dropped lp and draw through.

Double triple crochet (dtr): Yo (3 times), insert hook in designated st or sp, yo, draw yarn through st or sp, [yo, draw yarn through 2 lps on hook] 4 times.

With A, ch 5, join with a Sl st to form a ring.

RND 1: With A, ch 4 (counts as 1 dc, ch 1), [1 dc, ch 1] 11 times in ring, join with a Sl st to 3rd ch of beg ch-4 (12 ch-1 sps).

RND 2: With A, ch 6, (counts as 1 dc, ch 3), *1 pc in next dc, ch 3**, 1 dc in next dc, ch 3, rep from * 4 times, rep from * to ** once, join with a Sl st in 3rd ch of beg ch-6 (6 pc, 6 dc, 12 ch-3 sps). Fasten off A.

RND 3: With RS facing, join B in first dc, ch 1, 1 sc in same st, ch 4, *1 sc in next pc, ch 4**, 1 sc in next dc, ch 4, rep from * 4 times, rep from * to ** once, join with a Sl st in first sc (12 ch-4 sps).

RND 4: With B, Sl st in next ch-4 sp, ch 2 (counts as 1 hdc), (1 dc, 1 tr, 1 dtr, 1 tr, 1 dc, 1 hdc) in same ch-4 sp, (1 hdc, 1 dc, 1 tr, 1 dtr, 1 tr, 1 dc, 1 hdc) in each ch-4 sp around, join with a Sl st in 2nd ch of beg ch-2 (12 petals). Fasten off B.

RND 5: With RS facing, join C in sp between last petal and first petal, ch 4 (counts as tr), 1 tr in same sp (half corner made), *ch 4, sk next 3 sts, 1 sc in next dtr, [ch 4, sk next 6 sts, 1 sc in next dtr] twice, ch 4, sk next 3 sts**, (2 tr, ch 3, 2 tr) in sp between last skipped petal and next petal, rep from * twice, rep from * to ** once, 2 tr in same sp as first half corner, ch 1, 1 hdc in 4th ch of beg ch-4 (completes corner).

RND 6: With C, ch 3, 1 dc in same sp (half corner), *ch 2, 4 sc in each of next 4 ch-4 sps, ch 2**, (2 dc, ch 3, 2 dc) in next ch-3 sp (corner), rep from * twice, rep from * to ** once, join with a Sl st in 3rd ch of beg ch-3 (completes corner). Fasten off C.

RND 7: With RS facing, join A in first dc, ch 1, starting in same st, *1 sc in each of next 2 dc, 1 sc in next ch-2 sp, 1 sc in each of next 16 sc, 1 sc in next ch-2 sp, 1 sc in each of next 2 dc, (2 sc, ch 1, 2 sc) in next ch-3 sp (corner made), rep from * 3 times, join with a Sl st in first sc. Fasten off.

50 | KALEIDOSCOPE

SKILL LEVEL: Intermediate

Made with 4 colors: A, B, C, and D.

Beginning cluster (beg cluster): Ch 3, [yo, insert hook in st or sp, yo, draw up a loop, yo, draw through 2 lps] twice in same st or sp, yo, draw through 3 loops on hook.

Cluster: [Yo, insert hook in st or sp, yo, draw up a loop, yo, draw through 2 loops on hook] 3 times in same st or sp, yo, draw through 4 loops on hook.

With A, ch 6, join with a Sl st to form a ring.

RND 1: With A, ch 4 (counts as dc, ch 1), [1 dc, ch 1] 7 times in ring, join with a Sl st in 3rd ch of beg ch-4 (8 ch-1 sps).

RND 2: With A, ch 3 (counts as dc here and throughout), 1 dc in next ch-1 sp, ch 2, (2 dc, ch 2) in each ch-1 sp around, join with a Sl st in 3rd ch of beg ch-3 (16 dc, 8 ch-1 sps). Fasten off A.

RND 3: With right side facing join B in any ch-1 sp, (beg cluster, ch 2, cluster) in first sp, ch 2 (cluster, ch 2, cluster, ch 2) in each ch-1 sp around, join with a Sl st in first cluster (8 clusters, 16 ch-2 sps). Drop B to wrong side.

RND 4: With right side facing, join C in first ch-2 sp, (beg cluster, ch 3, cluster) in first ch-2 sp, ch 3, sk next ch-2 sp, *[1 cluster, ch 3] 3 times in next ch-2 sp, sk next ch-2 sp**, [1 cluster, ch 3] twice in next ch-2 sp, sk next ch-2 sp, rep from * twice, rep from * to ** once, join with a Sl st in 3rd ch of beg ch-3 (4 groups of 3 clusters, 4 groups of 2 clusters). Fasten off C.

RND 5: With right side facing, join A in first ch-3 sp between 2-cluster group, ch 3, 2 dc in same sp (half corner made), *ch 2, 2 dc in next ch-3 sp, (ch 1, 1 sc) in each of next 2 ch-3 sp, ch 1, 2 dc in next ch-3 sp, ch 2**, (3 dc, ch 3, 3 dc) in next ch-3 sp (corner), rep from * twice, rep from * to ** once, 3 dc in same sp as first half corner, ch 3, join with a Sl st in 3rd ch of beg ch-3. Drop A to wrong side, pick up B.

RND 6: With B, ch 1, starting in same st, *1 sc in each of next 3 dc, 2 sc in next ch-2 sp, 1 sc in each of next 2 dc, [1 sc in next ch-1 sp, 1 sc in next sc] twice, 1 sc in next ch-1 sp, 1 sc in each of next 2 dc, 2 sc in next ch-2 sp, 1 sc in each of next 3 dc, (1 sc, ch 3, 1 sc) in next ch-3 sp (corner made), rep from * around, join with a Sl st in first sc. Fasten off B. Pick up C and draw through loop on hook.

RND 7: With C, ch 1, *1 sc in each sc across to next corner, (1 sc, ch 3, 1 sc) in next ch-3 sp, rep from * 3 times, 1 sc in next sc, join with a Sl st in first sc (23 sc between each corner ch-3 sp). Fasten off C. Pick up A and draw through loop on hook.

RND 8: With A, ch 1, *1 sc in each sc across to next corner, (1 sc, ch 3, 1 sc) in next ch-3 sp, rep from * 3 times, 1 sc in each of next 2 sc, join with a Sl st in first sc (25 sc between each corner. Fasten off A.

51 | NAUTICAL WHEEL

SKILL LEVEL: Intermediate

Made with 2 colors: A and B.

Beginning cluster (beg cluster): Ch 3, [yo, insert hook in st or sp, yo, draw up a loop, yo, draw through 2 loops] twice in same st or sp, yo, draw through 3 loops on hook.

Cluster: [Yo, insert hook in st or sp, yo, draw up a loop, yo, draw through 2 loops on hook] 3 times in same st or sp, yo, draw through 4 loops on hook.

Picot: Ch 3, hdc in last hdc made.

With A, ch 6, join with a Sl st to form a ring.

RND 1: With A, ch 6 (counts as a tr, ch 2), [1 tr, ch 2] 11 times in ring, join with a Sl st to 3rd ch of beg ch-6 (12 ch-2 sps).

RND 2: With A, Sl st in next ch-2 sp, beg cluster in same sp, ch 3, (cluster, ch 3) in each ch-2 sp around, join with a Sl st in 3rd ch of beg ch-3 (12 clusters).

RND 3: With A, Sl st in next ch-3 sp, ch 2 (counts as hdc), [1 hdc, picot, 2 hdc] in same ch-3 sp (petal made), (3 hdc, picot, 2 hdc) in each ch-3 sp around, join with a Sl st in 2nd ch of beg ch-2 (12 petals). Fasten off A.

RND 4: With right side facing, join B between last hdc and first hdc of last rnd, ch 4 (counts as tr), 2 tr in same sp between 2 dc (half corner made), *[ch 3, sk next petal, 2 dc between skipped petal and next petal] twice, ch 3, sk next petal**, (3 tr, ch 3, 3 tr) in next sp between petals, rep from * twice, rep from * to ** once, 3 tr in same sp as beg half corner, ch 3, join with Sl st in 4th ch beg ch-4 (completes corner). Drop B to wrong side, pick up A.

RND 5: With A, ch 1, starting in same st, *1 sc in each of next 3 tr, [3 sc in ch-3 sp, 1 sc in each of next 2 dc] twice, 3 sc in next ch-3 sp, 1 sc in each of next 3 tr, (1 sc, ch 3, 1 sc) in next ch-3 sp (corner made), rep from * around, join with a Sl st in first sc. Fasten off A. Pick up B and draw through loop on hook.

RND 6: With B, ch 1, starting in same st, *1 sc in each sc to corner ch-3 sp, (2 sc, ch 2, 2 sc) in ch-3 sp, repeat from * 3 times, sc in next sc, join with a Sl st in first sc. Fasten off B.

52 | DEVON CROSS

SKILL LEVEL: Beginner

Ch 6, join with a Sl st to form a ring.

RND 1: Ch 3 (counts as dc here and throughout), 4 dc in ring, ch 8 [5 dc, ch 8] 3 times in ring, join with a Sl st in 3rd ch of beg ch-3 (4 ch-8 sps).

RND 2: Sl st in next 4 dc and in next ch-8 sp, ch 3, (2 dc, ch 3, 3 dc) in same sp, ch 5, *(3 dc, ch 3, 3 dc) in next ch-8 sp, ch 5, rep from * twice, join with Sl st in 3rd ch of beg ch-3.

RND 3: Ch 3, 1 dc in each of next 2 dc, *(3 dc, ch 3, 3 dc) in next ch-3 sp, 1 dc in each of next 3 dc, ch 2, 1 sc in center ch of next ch-5 sp, ch 2**, 1 dc in each of next 3 dc, rep from * twice, rep from * to ** once, join with a Sl st in 3rd ch of beg ch-3.

RND 4: Ch 3, 1 dc in each of next 5 dc, *(3 dc, ch 3, 3 dc) in next ch-3 sp, 1 dc in each of next 6 dc, ch 5, sk next 2 ch-2 sps**, 1 dc in each of next 6 dc, rep from * twice, rep from * to ** once, join with a Sl st in 3rd ch of beg ch-3.

RND 5: Ch 3, 1 dc in each of next 8 dc, *(3 dc, ch 3, 3 dc) in next ch-3 sp, 1 dc in each of next 9 dc, ch 2, 1 sc in 3rd ch of next ch-5 sp, ch 2**, 1 dc in each of next 9 dc, rep from * twice, rep from * to ** once, join with a Sl st in 3rd ch of beg ch-3.

RND 6: Ch 1, starting in same st, *1 sc in each of next 12 dc, (2 sc, ch 3, 2 sc) in next ch-3 sp, 1 sc in each of next 12 dc, 2 sc in next ch-2 sp, 1 sc in next sc, 2 sc in next ch-2 sp, rep from * around, join with a Sl st in first sc. Fasten off.

53 | CHRISTIANE SQUARE

SKILL LEVEL: Beginner

Made with 3 colors: A, B, and C.

With A, ch 8, join with a Sl st to form a ring.

RND 1: With A, ch 3 (counts as dc here and throughout), 23 dc in ring, join with a Sl st in 3rd ch of beg ch-3 (24 dc). Fasten off A.

RND 2: With right side facing, join B in any dc, ch 3, 1 dc in each of next 2 dc, ch 5, sk next st, *1 dc in each of next 3 dc, ch 5, sk next dc, rep from * 4 times, join with a Sl st in 3rd ch of beg ch-3 (6 ch-5 sps).

RND 3: With B, ch 1, starting in same st, 1 sc in each of next 3 dc, *(2 sc, ch 2, 2 sc) in next ch-5 sp, rep from * 5 times, join with a Sl st in first sc (6 ch-2 sps). Fasten off B.

RND 4: With right side facing, join C in first st, ch 3, 1 dc in each of next 4 sc, 3 dc in next ch-2 sp, *1 dc in each of next 7 sc, 3 dc in next ch-2 sp, rep from * 4 times, 1 dc in each of next 2 sc, join with a Sl st in 3rd ch of beg ch-3 (60 dc).

RND 5: With C, ch 3, 1 dc in each of next 3 dc, ch 6, sk next 5 dc, *1 dc in each of next 5 dc, ch 6, sk next 5 dc, rep from * 4 times, 1 dc in next dc, join with a Sl st in 3rd ch of beg ch-3 (6 ch-5 sps). Fasten off C.

RND 6: With right side facing, join B in first st, ch 1, starting in same st, 1 sc in each of next 4 dc, *[2 sc in next ch-5 space, working over ch-5 space, 1 sc in center dc on group of 3 dc in Rnd 3, 2 sc in same ch-5 space], (2 hdc, ch 2, 2 hdc) in next dc (corner made), 1 sc in each of next 4 dc, rep bet [ ] once, 1 sc in each of next 4 dc, (2 hdc, ch 2, 2 hdc) in next dc (corner made), rep bet [ ] once*, 1 sc in next 5 dc, rep from * to * once, 1 sc in next sc, join with a Sl st in first sc (4 ch-2 corner spaces). Fasten off B.

RND 7: With right side facing, join A in any corner ch-2 sp, ch 1, *(2 sc, ch 1, 2 sc) in corner ch-2 sp (corner made), 1 sc in each sc across to next corner ch-2 sp, rep from * 3 times, join with a Sl st in first sc (4 ch-2 corner sps). Fasten off A.

RND 8: With B, rep rnd 7. Fasten off B.

RND 9: With C rep rnd 7. Fasten off C.

54 | POPCORN SQUARE

SKILL LEVEL: Intermediate

Made with 3 colors: A, B, and C.

Beginning popcorn (beg pc): Ch 2, work 4 hdc in designated st, remove hook from last loop, place hook from front to back in top of the first of last 5 dc, pick up dropped loop, draw through loop on hook to complete pc.

Popcorn (pc): Work 5 hdc in designated st, remove hook from last loop, place hook from front to back in top of the first of last 5 dc, pick up dropped loop, draw through loop on hook to complete pc.

With A, ch 10, join with a Sl st to form a ring.

RND 1: With A, ch 1, work 16 sc in ring, join with a Sl st in first sc (16 sc).

RND 2: With A, beg pc in first sc, ch 3, sk next sc, *pc in next sc, ch 3, sk next sc, rep from * 6 times, join with a Sl st in beg pc (8 pc, 8 ch-3 sps). Fasten off A.

RND 3: With right side facing, join B in any pc, ch 1, 1 sc in same st, (ch 6, 1 sc) in each pc around, ch 3, 1 dc in first sc instead of last ch-6 sp (8 ch-6 sps).

RND 4: With B, ch 3 (counts as dc), 4 dc in same sp (half corner), *ch 3, 1 sc in next ch-6 sp, ch 3**, (5 dc, ch 3, 5 dc) in next ch-6 sp (corner), rep from * twice, rep from * to ** once, join with a Sl st in 3rd ch of beg ch-3 (completes corner).

RND 5: With B, ch 7 (counts as 1 dc, ch 4), *1 sc in next ch-3 sp, ch 3, 1 sc in next ch-3 sp, ch 4**, (5 dc, ch 3, 5 dc) in next ch-3 sp (corner made), ch 4, rep from * twice, rep from * to ** once, (5 dc, ch 3, 4 dc) in next ch-3 sp, join with a Sl st in 3rd ch of beg ch-6 (completes corner). Fasten off B.

RND 6: With right side facing, join C in any ch-3 corner sp, ch 3, 2 dc in same sp (half corner made), *(ch 2, 3 dc) in each of next 3 ch-sps, ch 2**, (3 dc, ch 3, 3 dc) in next ch-3 sp (corner made), rep from * twice, rep from * to ** once, join with a Sl st in 3rd ch of beg ch-3 (completes corner). Fasten off.

55 | POPCORNS AND LACE

SKILL LEVEL: Intermediate

Beginning cluster (beg cluster): Ch 3, [yo (twice), insert hook in st or sp, yo, draw up a loop, yo, draw through 2 loops] 3 times in same st or sp, yo, draw through 4 loops on hook.

Cluster: [Yo (twice), insert hook in st or space, yo, draw up a loop, yo, draw through 2 lps] 4 times in same st or space, yo, draw through 5 loops on hook.

Beginning popcorn (beg pc): Ch 3 (counts as dc), 4 dc in same st or sp, drop loop from hook, insert hook in the 3rd ch of beg ch-3, pick up the dropped loop and draw through.

Popcorn (pc): Work 5 dc in same st or sp, drop loop from hook, insert hook in the first of the 5 dc just made, pick up dropped loop and draw through.

Ch 8, join with a Sl st to form a ring.

RND 1: Beg cluster in ring, *ch 3, 1 cluster in ring, ch 5**, 1 cluster in ring, rep from * twice, rep from * to ** once, join with a Sl st in 3rd ch of beg ch-3 (8 clusters, 4 ch-3 sps, 4 ch-5 sps).

RND 2: Sl st to center of next ch-3 sp, ch 1, 1 sc in same sp, *9 tr in the next ch-5 sp, 1 sc in next ch-3 sp, rep from * around, omit last sc, join with a Sl st in first sc (4 groups of 9 tr).

RND 3: Beg pc in first sc, *ch 2, sk next 2 tr, 1 dc in next tr, ch 2, sk next tr, (2 dc, ch 3, 2 dc) in next tr, ch 2, sk next tr, 1 dc in next tr, ch 2, sk next 2 tr**, 1 pc in next sc, rep from * twice, rep from * to ** once, join with a Sl st in top of first pc.

RND 4: Ch 3 (counts as dc), *[2 dc in ch-2 sp, 1 dc in next dc] twice, 1 dc in next dc, (2 dc, ch 3, 2 dc) in next ch-3 sp, 1 dc in next dc [1 dc in next dc, 2 dc in ch-2 sp] twice**, 1 dc in next pc, rep from * twice, rep from * to ** once, join with a Sl st in 3rd ch of beg ch-3.

RND 5: Ch 6 (counts as dc, ch 3), 1 dc in same st at base of ch-6, *sk next 2 dc, 1 dc in each of next 3 dc, 1 pc in next dc, 1 dc in each of next 3 dc, (2 dc, ch 3, 2 dc) in next ch-3 sp, 1 dc in each of next 3 dc, 1 pc in next dc, 1 dc in each of next 3 dc, sk next 2 dc**, (1 dc, ch 3, 1 dc) in next dc, rep from * twice, rep from * to ** once, join with a Sl st in 3rd ch of beg ch-6.

RND 6: Sl st to 2nd ch of next ch-3 sp, ch 4 (counts as dc, ch 1), *sk next dc, 1 dc in next dc, [ch 1, sk next st, 1 dc in next st] 4 times, (2 dc, ch 3, 2 dc) in next ch-3 sp, [1 dc in next dc, ch 1, sk next st] 5 times**, 1 dc in 2nd ch of next ch-3 sp, ch 1, rep from * twice, rep from * to ** once, join with a Sl st in 3rd ch of beg ch-4. Fasten off.

THE GRANNY SQUARE BOOK

56 | POPCORNS AND SHELLS

SKILL LEVEL: Experienced

Popcorn (pc): Work 5 hdc in designated st, remove hook from last loop, place hook from front to back in top of the first of last 5 dc, pick up dropped loop, draw through loop on hook to complete pc.

Ch 6, join with a Sl st to form a ring.

RND 1: Ch 3 (counts as dc here and thoughout), 1 dc in ring, (ch 3, 3 dc in ring) 3 times, ch 3, 1 dc in ring, join with a Sl st in 3rd ch of beg ch-3 (4 ch-3 sps).

RND 2: Ch 3, *1 pc in next st, 5 dc in next ch-3 sp, 1 pc in next dc**, 1 dc in next dc, rep from * twice, rep from * to ** once, join with a Sl st in 3rd ch of beg ch-3 (8 pc).

RND 3: Ch 5 (counts as dc, ch 2 here and throughout), *sk next pc, 1 pc in next dc, 1 dc in next dc, 3 dc in next dc, 1 dc in next dc, 1 pc in next dc, ch 2, sk next pc**, 1 dc in next dc, ch 2, rep from * twice, rep from * to ** once, join with a Sl st in 3rd ch of beg ch-5 (8 ch-2 sps).

RND 4: Sl st in next ch-2 sp, ch 5, *sk next pc, 1 pc in next dc, 1 dc in next dc, 3 dc in next dc, 1 dc in next dc, 1 pc in next dc, ch 2, sk next pc**, [1 dc in next ch-2 sp, ch 2] twice, rep from * twice, rep from * to ** once, 1 dc in next ch-2 sp, ch 2, join with a Sl st in 3rd ch of beg ch-5 (12 ch-2 sps).

RND 5: Sl st in next ch-2 sp, ch 5, *sk next pc, 1 pc in next dc, 1 dc in next dc, 3 dc in next dc, 1 pc in next dc, ch 2,** [1 dc in next ch-2 sp, ch 2] 3 times, rep from * twice, rep from * to ** once, [1 dc in next ch-2 sp, ch 2] twice, join with a Sl st in 3rd ch of beg ch-5 (16 ch-2 sps).

RND 6: Sl st in next ch-2 sp, ch 5, *sk next pc, 1 pc in next dc, 1 dc in next dc, 3 dc in next dc, 1 pc in next dc, ch 2,** [1 dc in next ch-2 sp, ch 2] 4 times, rep from * twice, rep from * to ** once, [1 dc in next ch-2 sp, ch 2] 3 times, join with a Sl st in 3rd ch of beg ch-5 (20 ch-2 sps).

RND 7: Ch 1, 1 sc in first st, *2 sc in next ch-2 sp, 1 sc in next pc, 1 sc in each of next 2 sts, (1 sc, ch 3, 1 sc) in next st (corner), 1 sc in each of next 2 sts, 1 sc in next pc, [2 sc in next ch-2 sp, 1 sc in next st] 4 times, rep from * 3 times, omitting last sc, join with a Sl st in first sc (4 ch-3 sps). Fasten off.

57 | EIGHT PETAL FLOWER

SKILL LEVEL: Intermediate

Made with 3 colors: A, B, and C.

With A, ch 6, join with a Sl st to form a ring.

RND 1: With A, ch 3 (counts as 1 dc here and throughout), 15 dc in ring, join with a Sl st in 3rd ch of beg ch-3 (16 dc).

RND 2: With A, ch 5 (counts as 1 dc, ch 2), 1 dc in same st as last Sl st (counts as V-st) *ch 1, sk next dc, (1 dc, ch 2, 1 dc) in next dc (V-st made), rep from * 6 times, ch 1, sk next dc, join with a Sl st in 3rd ch of the beg ch-5 (8 V-sts made).

RND 3: With A, Sl st in next ch-2 sp, ch 3, (1 dc, ch 2, 2 dc) in same ch-2 sp, *ch 1, sk next ch-1 sp, (2 dc, ch 2, 2 dc) in the next ch-2 sp, rep from * 6 times, ch 1, sk next ch-1 sp, Sl st in 3rd ch of beg ch-3 (8 shells). Fasten off A.

RND 4: With right side facing, join B in any ch-2 sp, ch 3, work 6 dc in first ch-2 sp, 1 sc in next ch-1 sp, *7 dc in next ch-2 sp, 1 sc in next ch-1 sp, rep from * 6 times, join with a Sl st in 3rd ch of beg ch-3 (8 shells). Fasten off B.

RND 5: With right side facing, join C in any sc, ch 3, 2 dc in same st (half corner made), *ch 3, sk next 3 dc, 1 sc in next dc, ch 3, sk next 3 dc, 1 dc in next sc, ch 3, sk next 3 dc, 1 sc in next dc, ch 3, sk next 3 dc**, (3 dc, ch 3, 3 dc) in next sc (corner), rep from * twice, rep from * to ** once, 3 dc in same sc as half corner, ch 3, join with a Sl st in 3rd ch of beg ch-3 (completes corner).

RND 6: With C, ch 1, starting in same st, *1 sc in each of next 3 dc, [3 sc in next ch-3 sp, 1 sc in next st] 3 times, 3 sc in next ch-3 sp, 1 sc in each of next 3 dc, (1 sc, ch 3, 1 sc) in next ch-3 sp (corner), rep from * 3 times, join with a Sl st in first sc. Fasten off.

58 | TUSCAN TILE

SKILL LEVEL: Intermediate

Made with 3 colors: A, B, and C.

With A, ch 4, join with a Sl st to form a ring.

RND 1: With A, ch 5 (counts as tr, ch 1), [1 tr, ch 1] 11 times in ring, join with a Sl st in 4th ch of beg ch-5 (12 ch-1 sp). Fasten off A.

RND 2: With right side facing, join B in any tr, ch 3 (counts as dc), (1 dc, ch 3, 2 dc) in same st as joining (corner made), *(ch 1, 1 dc) in each of next 2 tr, ch 1**, (2 dc, ch 3, 2 dc) in next tr (corner made), rep from * twice, rep from * to ** once, ch 1, join with a Sl st in 3rd ch of beg ch-3 (4 ch-3 sps, 12 ch-1 sps). Fasten off B.

RND 3: With right side facing, join C in any ch-3 corner sp, ch 2, (1 hdc, ch 3, 2 hdc) in same sp (corner made), *1 hdc in each of next 2 dc, working over next ch-1 sp in rnd 2, 1 tr in next ch-1 sp in rnd 1, 1 sc in each of next 2 dc, working over next ch-1 sp in rnd 2, 1 tr in next ch-1 sp in rnd 1, 1 hdc in each of next 2 dc**, (2 hdc, ch 3, 2 hdc) in next ch-3 sp (corner made), rep from * twice, rep from * to ** once, join with Sl st in 2nd ch of beg ch-2 (4 ch-2 sps). Fasten off C.

RND 4: With right side facing, join B in any ch-3 corner sp, ch 1, *(1 sc, ch 2, 1 sc) in ch-2 corner sp (corner made), 1 sc in each of next 12 sts, rep from * 3 times, join with a Sl st in first sc (4 ch-2 sps). Fasten off B.

RND 5: With right side facing, join C in any ch-3 corner sp, ch 1, *(1 sc, ch 2, 1 sc) in ch-2 corner sp (corner made), 1 sc in each of next 14 sts, rep from * 3 times, join with a Sl st in first sc (4 ch-2 sps).

RND 6: With C, Sl st in next ch-3 corner sp, ch 3, (1 dc, ch 2, 2 dc) in same sp (corner made), *[ch 1, sk next sc, 1 dc in each of next 2 sc] 5 times, ch 1**, (2 dc, ch 2, 2 dc) in next corner ch-2 sp (corner made), rep from * twice, rep from * to ** once, join with a Sl st in 3rd ch of beg ch-3 (completes corner) (4 ch-2 sps, 24 ch-1 sps). Fasten off C.

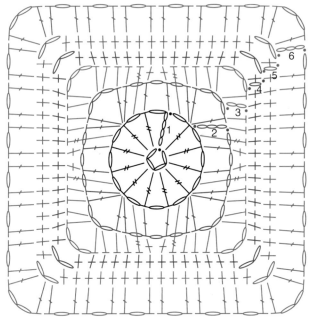

59 | POINSETTIA SQUARE

SKILL LEVEL: Intermediate

Double crochet 2 together (dc2tog): [Yo, insert hook in next st, yo, draw yarn though st, yo, draw yarn through 2 loops on hook] twice, yo, draw yarn through 3 loops on hook.

Double crochet 5 together (dc5tog): [Yo, insert hook in next st, yo, draw yarn though st, yo, draw yarn through 2 loops on hook] 5 times, yo, draw yarn through 6 loops on hook.

Ch 6, join with a Sl st to form a ring.

RND 1: Ch 3 (counts as dc here and throughout), 15 dc in ring, join with a Sl st in 3rd ch of beg ch-3 (16 dc).

RND 2: Ch 4 (counts as dc, ch 1 here and throughout), *5 dc in next dc, ch 1**, 1 dc in next dc, ch 1, rep from * 6 times, rep from * to ** once, join with a Sl st in 3rd ch of beg ch-4 (12 ch-1 sps).

RND 3: Ch 4, 1 dc in first st, *ch 1, 2 dc in each of next 5 dc, ch 1**, (1 dc, ch 1, 1 dc) in next dc, ch 1, rep from * 6 times, rep from * to ** once, join with a Sl st in 3rd ch of beg ch-4 (24 ch-1 sps).

RND 4: Ch 3, 1 dc in first st, ch 1, 2 dc in next dc, ch 1, *(dc2tog in next 2 sts) 5 times, ch 1**, (2 dc in next dc, ch 1) twice, rep from * 6 times, rep from * to ** once, join with a Sl st in 3rd ch of beg ch-3 (24 ch-1 sps).

RND 5: Ch 4, (1 dc, ch 1) in each of next 3 dc, *dc5tog worked across next 5 sts, ch 1**, (1 dc, ch 1) in each of next 4 dc, rep from * 6 times, rep from * to ** once, join with a Sl st in 3rd ch of beg ch-4 (40 ch-1 sps).

RND 6: Ch 4, *1 dc in next dc, ch 1, (2 tr, ch 3, 2 tr) into next ch-1 sp, (ch 1, 1 dc) in each of next 2 dc, ch 1, 1 hdc in next dc5tog, (ch 1, 1 sc) in each of next 4 dc, ch 1, 1 hdc in next dc5tog, ch 1**, 1 dc in next dc, ch 1, rep from * twice, rep from * to ** once, join with a Sl st in 3rd ch of beg ch-4 (44 ch-1 sps, 4 ch-3 sps).

RND 7: Ch 3, *1 dc in next ch-1 sp, 1 dc in next dc, 1 dc in next ch-1 sp, 1 dc in each of next 2 tr, (2 dc, ch 2, 2 dc) in next ch-3 sp, 1 dc in each of next 2 tr, (1 dc in ch-1 sp, 1 dc in next dc) twice, 1 dc in next ch-1 sp, 1 dc in next hdc, (1 dc in next ch-1 sp, 1 dc in next sc) 4 times, 1 dc in next ch-1 sp, 1 dc in next hdc, 1 dc in next ch-1 sp, 1 dc in next dc, rep from * around, omitting 1 dc at end of last rep, join with a Sl st in 3rd ch of beg ch-3 (4 ch-2 sps). Fasten off.

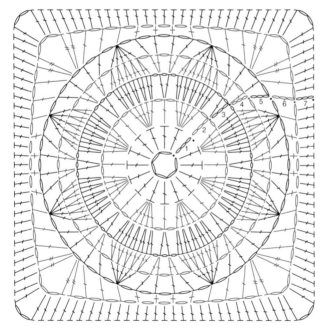

60 | FLORENTINE TILE

SKILL LEVEL: Experienced

Made with 3 colors: A, B, and C.

With A, ch 6, join with a Sl st to form a ring.

RND 1: With A, ch 1, 16 sc in ring, join with a Sl st in first sc (16 sc).

RND 2: Ch 6 (counts as dc, ch 3), dc in same st (corner made), *ch 1, sk next sc, dc in next sc, ch 1, sk next sc **, (dc, ch 3, dc) in next sc (corner made), rep from * twice, rep from * to ** once, join with a Sl st in 3rd ch of beg ch 6 (4 ch-3 sps, 8 ch-1 sps). Fasten off A.

RND 3: With right side facing, join B in any ch-3 corner sp, ch 1, 5 sc in same sp, *[1 sc in next dc, working behind next ch-1 sp, 1 dc in next skipped st 2 rnds below] twice, 1 sc in next dc**, 5 sc in next ch-3 corner sp, rep from * twice, rep from * to ** once, join with a Sl st in first sc.

RND 4: With B, ch 4, (counts as dc, ch 1 here and throughout), sk next st, *(dc, ch 3, dc) in next st (corner made)**, (ch 1, sk next st, dc in next st) 4 times, ch 1, sk next st, rep from * twice, rep from * to ** once, (ch 1, sk next st, dc in next st) 3 times, ch 1, sk last st, join with a Sl st in 3rd ch of beg ch-4. Fasten off B.

RND 5: With right side facing, join C in any ch-3 corner sp, ch 1, 5 sc in same sp, *[1 sc in next st, working behind next ch-1 sp, dc in next skipped st 2 rnds below] 5 times, sc in next st **, 5 sc in next corner ch-3 sp, rep from * twice, rep from * to ** once, join with a Sl st in first sc.

RND 6: With C, ch 4, sk next st, *(dc, ch 3, dc) in next st (corner made)**, [ch 1, sk next st, dc in next st] 7 times, ch 1, sk next st, rep from * twice, rep from * to ** once, [ch 1, sk next st, dc in next st] 6 times, ch 1, sk last st, join with a Sl st in 3rd ch of beg ch-4 (32 ch-1 sps, 4 ch-3 sps). Fasten off C.

RND 7: With right side facing, join B in any ch-3 corner sp, ch 1, 5 sc in same sp (corner made), *[1 sc in next st, working behind next ch-1 sp, dc in next skipped st 2 rnds below] 8 times, sc in next st**, 5 sc in next corner ch-3 sp, rep from * twice, rep from * to ** once, join with a Sl st in first sc. Fasten off B.

RND 8: With right side facing, join A in center st of any corner, ch 3 (counts as dc), 1 dc in same st (half corner made), *[ch 1, sk next st, 1 dc in next st] 10 times, ch 1**, sk next st, (2 dc, ch 3, 2 dc) in next st (corner made), rep from * twice, rep from * to ** once, sk next st, 2 dc in same st as first half corner, ch 3, join with a Sl st to 3rd ch of beg ch-3 (completes corner). Fasten off A.

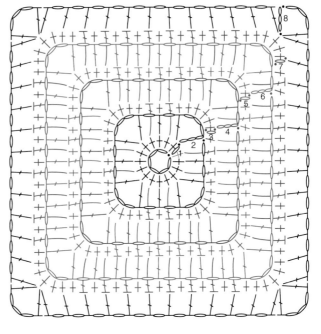

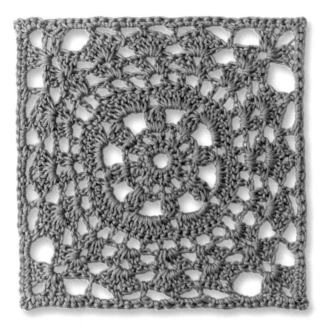

61 | ISABELLA SQUARE

SKILL LEVEL: Intermediate

Beginning Cluster (beg cluster): Ch 3, [yo, insert hook in st or sp, yo, draw up a loop, yo, draw through 2 loops] twice in same st or sp, yo, draw through 3 loops on hook.

Cluster: [Yo, insert hook in st or sp, yo, draw up a loop, yo, draw through 2 loops on hook] 3 times in same st or sp, yo, draw through 4 loops on hook.

Ch 6, join with a Sl st to form a ring.

RND 1: Ch 1, 16 sc in ring, join with a Sl st to first sc (16 sc).

RND 2: Ch 4 (counts as dc, ch 1), 1 dc in same st (V-st made), ch 1, sk next sc, *(1 dc, ch 1, 1 dc) in next sc, ch 1, sk 1 sc, rep from * 6 times, join with a Sl st in 3rd ch of beg ch-3 (8 V-sts).

RND 3: Sl st in next ch-1 sp, beg cluster in same sp, ch 5, sk next ch-1 sp, *1 cluster in next ch-1 sp, ch 5, sk next ch-1 sp, rep from * around, join with a Sl st in top of beg cluster (8 clusters).

RND 4: Sl st in next ch-5 sp, ch 3 (counts as dc here and throughout), 7 dc in same ch-5 sp, 8 dc in each ch-5 sp around, join with a Sl st in 3rd ch of beg ch-3 (64 dc).

RND 5: Ch 4 (counts as dc, ch 1 here and throughout), sk next dc, *1 dc in next dc, ch 1, sk next st, rep from * 30 times, join with a Sl st in 3rd ch of beg ch-4 (32 ch-1 sps).

RND 6: Sl st in next ch-1 sp, ch 3, (1 dc, ch 1, 2 dc) in same ch-1 sp (shell made), *ch 1, sk next ch-1 sp**, (2 dc, ch 1, 2 dc) in next ch-1 sp (shell made), rep from * 14 times, rep from * to ** once, join with a Sl st in 3rd ch of beg ch-3 (16 shells).

RND 7: Sl st in next dc and in next ch-1 sp, ch 3, (2 dc ch 1, 3 dc) in same sp (shell made), *ch 1, sk next ch-1 sp** (3 dc, ch 1, 3 dc) in next ch-1 sp of next shell (shell made), rep from * 14 times, rep from * to ** once, join with a Sl st in 3rd ch of beg ch-3 (16 shells).

RND 8: Sl st in next 2 dc, and in next ch-1 sp, ch 3, (2 dc, ch 3, 3 dc) in same sp (corner made), sk next ch-1 sp, *[ch 3, 1 sc in ch-1 sp of next shell, ch 3, hdc in next ch-1 sp] 3 times, ch 3**, (3 dc, ch 3, 3 dc) in next ch-1 sp of next shell, rep from * twice, rep from * to ** once, join with a Sl st in 3rd ch of beg ch-3.

RND 9: Ch 1, starting in same st, *1 sc in each of next 3 dc, (2 sc, ch 3, 2 sc) in next ch-3 sp, 1 sc in each of next 3 dc, 3 sc in each of next 7 ch-3 sps, rep from * around, join with a Sl st in first sc. Fasten off.

62 | PRETTY POSY

SKILL LEVEL: Intermediate

Made with 3 colors, A, B, and C.

With A, ch 8, join with a Sl st to form a ring.

RND 1: With A, ch 3 (counts as dc here and throughout), 1 dc in ring, ch 3, [2 dc, ch 3] 7 times in ring, join with a Sl st in 3rd ch of beg ch-3 (8 ch-3 sps). Fasten off A.

RND 2: With right side facing, join B in any ch-3 sp, *ch 1, 3 tr in sp between next 2 dc, ch 1, Sl st into next ch-3 sp, rep from * 7 times, ending with last Sl st in same ch-3 sp as joining (8 groups of 3 tr). Fasten off B.

RND 3: With right side facing, working over sts in rnd 2, join C with a Sl st in any ch-3 sp in rnd 1, ch 3, 2 dc in same ch-3 sp, *ch 3, Sl st in next ch-3 sp in rnd 1, ch 3**, 3 dc in next ch-3 sp in rnd 1, rep from * twice, rep from * to ** once, join with a Sl st in 3rd ch of beg ch-3 (4 groups of 3 dc, 8 ch-3 sps). Fasten off C.

RND 4: With right side facing, join A between the 2nd and 3rd dc in any 3-dc group, ch 3, 2 dc in same sp, 3 dc in each of next 2 ch-3 sps, 3 dc in sp between next 2 dc, ch 3**, 3 dc in between next 2 dc, rep from * twice, rep from * to ** once, join with a Sl st in 3rd ch of beg ch-3 (4 ch-3 sps). Fasten off A.

RND 5: With right side facing, join C in any ch-3 sp, ch 3, (1 dc, ch 3, 2 dc) in same sp (corner made), *1 dc in each of next 12 dc**, (2 dc, ch 3, 2 dc) in next ch-3 sp (corner made), rep from * twice, rep from * to ** once, join with a Sl st in 3rd ch of beg ch-3 (4 ch-3 sps). Fasten off C.

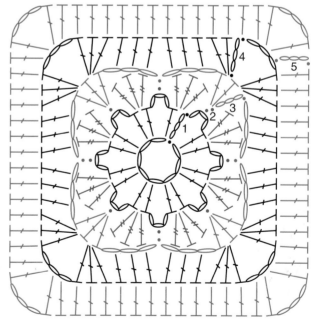

63 | FILIGREE ROSETTE

SKILL LEVEL: Intermediate

Made with 3 colors: A, B, and C.

With A, ch 4, join with a Sl st to form a ring.

RND 1: With A, 8 sc in ring, join with a Sl st in first sc (8 sc).

RND 2: With A, ch 5 (counts as dc ch-2), (1 dc, ch 2) in each sc around, join with a Sl st to 3rd ch of beg ch-5 (8 ch-2 sps). Fasten off A.

RND 3: With right side facing, join B in any ch-2 sp, ch 4 (counts as tr), 2 tr in same sp, ch 1, (3 tr, ch 1) in each ch-2 sp around, join with a Sl st in 4th ch of beg ch-4 (8 ch-1 sps). Fasten off B.

RND 4: With right side facing, join C in first tr of any group, ch 1, sc in same tr, *(1 sc, ch 3, 1 sc) in next tr, 1 sc in next tr, (1 sc, ch 8, 1 sc) in next ch-1 sp**, 1 sc in next tr, rep from * 6 times, rep from * to ** once, join with a Sl st in first sc. Fasten off C (8 ch-8 loops, 8 ch-3 sps).

RND 5: With right side facing, rejoin C in any ch-8 loop, ch 3 (counts as dc), (3 dc, ch 3, 4 dc) in same loop (corner made), *ch 2, 1 dc in next ch-3 sp, ch 2, 1 sc in next ch-8 loop, ch 2, 1 dc in next ch-3 loop, ch 2**, (4 dc, ch 3, 4 dc) in next ch-8 loop, rep from* twice, rep from * to ** once, join with a Sl st in 3rd ch of beg ch-3.

RND 6: With C, ch 1, starting in same st, 1 sc in each of next 4 dc *(2 sc, ch 2, 2 sc) in next ch 3-sp, 1 sc in each of next 4 dc, [2 sc in next ch-2 sp, 1 sc next st] 3 times, 2 dc in next ch-2 sp, 1 sc in each of next 4 dc, rep from * 3 times, join with a Sl st in first sc. Fasten off.

64 | ERICA SQUARE

SKILL LEVEL: Experienced

Made with 3 colors: A, B, and C.

Front post double crochet (FPdc): Yo, insert hook from front to back to front again around the post of next st, yo, draw yarn through, (yo, draw yarn through 2 loops on hook) twice.

Back post double crochet (BPdc): Yo, insert hook from back to front to back again around the post of next st, yo, draw yarn through, (yo, draw yarn through 2 loops on hook) twice.

With A, ch 8, join with a Sl st to form a ring.

RND 1: With A, ch 6 (counts as 1 dc, ch 3 here and throughout), [3 dc, ch 3] 3 times in ring, 2 dc in ring, Sl st in 3rd ch of beg ch-6 (4 ch-3 sps). Fasten off A.

RND 2: With right side facing, join B in a different ch-3 corner sp than first joining, ch 3 (counts as dc), 2 dc in same sp (half corner made), * 1 FPdc in each of next 3 sts**, (3 dc, ch 3, 3 dc) in next ch-3 sp (corner made), rep from * twice, rep from * to ** once, 3 dc in same sp as first half corner, join with a Sl st in 3rd ch of beg ch-3 (completes corner). Fasten off B.

RND 3: With right side facing, join C in a different ch-3 corner sp than joining, ch 6, 3 dc in same corner sp, *1 BPdc in each of next 3 sts, 1 FPdc in each of next 3 sts, 1 BPdc in each of next 3 sts**, (3 dc, ch 3, 3 dc) in next sp, rep from * twice, rep from * to ** once, 2 dc in same sp as first half corner, join with a Sl st in 3rd ch of beg ch-6 (completes corner) (4 ch-3 sps). Fasten off C.

RND 4: With right side facing, join A in a different corner sp than joining, ch 3 (counts as dc), 2 dc in same corner sp (half corner made), *1 dc in each of next 15 sts, **(3 dc, ch 3, 3 dc) in next ch-3 corner sp, rep from * twice, rep from * to ** once, 3 dc in same sp as first half corner, ch 3, join with a Sl st in 3rd ch of beg ch-3 (completes corner) (4 ch-3 sps). Fasten off A.

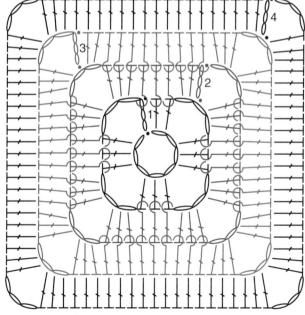

65 | MARIANNE SQUARE

SKILL LEVEL: Easy

Made with 3 colors: A, B, and C.

With A, ch 4, join with a Sl st to form a ring.

RND 1: With A, ch 3 (counts as dc here and throughout), 2 dc in ring, ch 2 (3 dc, ch 2) 3 times in ring, join with a Sl st in 3rd ch of beg ch-3 (4 ch-2 corner sps).

RND 2: With A, Sl st in each of next 2 dc and in next ch-3 sp, ch 8 (counts as dc, ch 5), dc in same sp (corner made), ch 5, *(dc, ch 5, dc) in each of next 3 ch-3 sps, ch 5, rep from * around, join with a Sl st in 3rd ch of beg ch-8 (8 ch-5 sps). Fasten off A.

RND 3: With right side facing, join B in any ch-5 corner sp, ch 3, (2 dc, ch 2, 3 dc) in same sp, *ch 2, 5 dc in next ch-5 sp, ch 2**, (3 dc, ch 2, 3 dc) in next ch-3 sp, rep from * twice, rep from * to ** once, join with a Sl st in 3rd ch of beg ch-3 (12 ch-2 sps). Fasten off B.

RND 4: With right side facing, join C in any ch-2 corner sp, ch 3, (2 dc, ch 2, 3 dc) in same sp (corner made), ch 1, 2 dc in next ch-2 sp, [1 dc between next 2 dc] 4 times, 2 dc in next ch-2 sp, ch 1**, (3 dc, ch 2, 3 dc) in next ch-3 sp (corner made), rep from * twice, rep from * to ** once, join with a Sl st in 3rd ch of beg ch-3 (8 ch-1 sps, 4 ch-2 sps).

RND 5: With C, ch 1, starting in same st, *1 sc in each of 3 dc, (2 sc, ch 2, 2 sc) in next ch-3 sp (corner made), 1 sc in each of next 3 dc, 1 sc in next ch-1 sp, 1 sc in each of next 8 dc, 1 sc in next ch-1 sp, rep from * 3 times, join with a Sl st in 3rd ch of beg ch-3 (4 ch-2 sps). Fasten off C.

RND 6: With right side facing, join A in any ch-3 corner sp, (1 dc, ch 3, 2 dc) in same sp (corner made), *1 dc in each of next 20 sc**, (2 dc, ch 3, 2 dc) in next ch-2 sp (corner made) rep from * twice, rep from * to ** once, join with a Sl st in 3rd ch of beg ch-3 (4 ch-3 sps). Fasten off A.

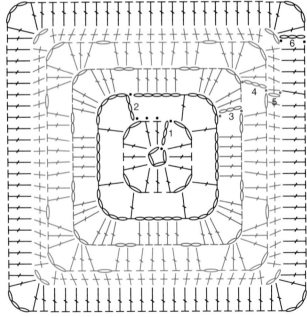

66 | SIX POINT STAR

SKILL LEVEL: Intermediate

Made with 3 colors: A, B, and C.

With A, ch 6, join with a Sl st to form a ring.

RND 1: With A, ch 1, (1 sc, ch 3) 12 times in ring, join with a Sl st in first sc (12 ch-3 sps).

RND 2: With A, Sl st in next 2 ch sts, ch 1, 1 sc in same ch-3 sp, (ch 3, 1 sc) in each ch-3 sp around, ch 1, 1 hdc in first sc to join instead of last ch-3 sp (12 ch-3 sps).

RND 3: With A, ch 1, 1 sc in same sp, *ch 6, 1 sc in next ch-3 sp **, ch 3, 1 sc in next ch-3 sp, rep from * 4 times, rep from * to ** once, ch 1, 1 hdc in first sc instead of last ch-3 sp (6 ch-6 sps, 6 ch-3 sps).

RND 4: Ch 1, 1 sc in same sp, *(5 dc, ch 2, 5 dc) in next ch-6 sp**, 1 sc in next ch-3 sp, rep from * 4 times, rep from * to ** once (6 ch-2 sps). Fasten off A.

RND 5: With right side facing, join B in any ch-2 sp, ch 1, 1 sc in same sp, *ch 6, 1 tr in next sc, ch 6**, 1 sc in next ch-2 sp, rep from * 4 times, rep from * to ** once, join with a Sl st in first sc (12 ch-6 sps).

RND 6: With B, Sl st in first 2 ch sts, ch 3 (counts as dc), 2 dc in same ch-6 sp, *ch 2, 3 dc in next ch-6 sp, ch 2, (3 dc, ch 3, 3 dc) in next ch-6 sp (corner made), ch 2**, 3 dc in next ch-6 sp, rep from * twice, rep from * to ** once, join with a Sl st in 3rd ch of beg ch-3 (12 ch-2 sps, 4 ch-3 sps). Fasten off B.

RND 7: With right side facing, join C in first st, ch 1, starting in same st, *1 sc in each of next 3 dc, [2 sc in next ch-2 sp, 1 dc in each of next 3 dc] twice, (2 sc, ch 2, 2 sc) in next ch-3 sp (corner made), 1 sc in each of next 3 dc, 2 sc in next ch-2 sp, rep from * 3 times, join with a Sl st in first sc (4 ch-2 sps). Fasten off C.

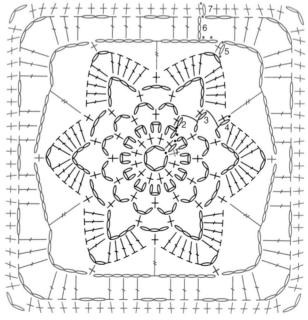

67 | QUARTET

SKILL LEVEL: Easy

Made with 2 colors: A and B.

Make 4 small squares, 2 each with A and B.

SQUARE:

Ch 8, join with a Sl st to form a ring.

RND 1: Ch 3, 3 tr in ring, ch 5, [4 tr, ch 5] 3 times in ring, join with a Sl st in 3rd ch of beg ch-3 (4 ch-5 sps). Fasten off.

ASSEMBLY:

Sew 4 squares together from the wrong side, through back loop only, alternating colors.

EDGING:

RND 1: With right side facing, join either color in any corner ch-5 sp, ch 3 (counts as dc), 2 dc in same sp (half corner made), *ch 2, sk next 2 dc, 1 dc between last skipped and next dc, [ch 2, 2 dc in next ch-5 sp] twice, ch 2, 1 dc between last skipped and next dc, ch 2**, (3 dc, ch 3, 3 dc) in next ch-5 sp, rep from * twice, rep from * to ** once, 3 dc in same ch-5 as first half corner, ch 3, join with a Sl st in 3rd ch of beg ch-3 (completes corner) (20 ch-2 sps, 4 ch-3 sps). Fasten off.

RND 2: With right side facing, join other color in any ch-3 corner sp, ch 1, 3 sc in same corner (half corner made), *1 sc in next 3 dc, 2 sc in next ch-2 sp, 1 sc in next dc, 2 sc in next ch-2 sp, 1 sc in each of next 2 dc, 2 sc in next ch-2 sp, 1 sc in each of next 2 dc, 2 sc in next ch-2 sp, 1 sc in next dc, 2 sc in next ch-2 sp, 1 sc in each of next 3 dc**, (3 sc, ch 2, 3 sc) in next ch-3 sp (corner made), rep from * twice, rep from * to ** once, 3 sc in same corner sp as first half corner, ch 2, join with a Sl st in first sc (completes corner) (4 ch-2 sps). Fasten off.

EDGING

68 | GRACIE SQUARE

SKILL LEVEL: Intermediate

Made with 3 colors: A, B, and C.

First 3 rounds of this pattern are worked from the wrong side.

With A, ch 4, join with a Sl st to form a ring.

RND 1 (WS): With A, ch 5 (counts as dc, ch 2), [1 dc, ch 2] 7 times in ring, join with a Sl st to 3rd ch of beg ch-5 (8 ch-2 sps).

RND 2 (WS): With A, *(Sl st, 2 dc, Sl st) in each ch-2 sp around, join with a Sl st in same place as first Sl st (8 groups of 2 dc).

RND 3 (WS): With A, ch 9 (counts as dc, ch 6), sk next 2 dc, *1 dc between next 2 Sl sts, ch 6, sk next 2 dc, rep from * 6 times, join with a Sl st in 3rd ch of beg ch-8, turn (8 ch-6 loops). Fasten off A.

RND 4: With right side facing, join B in first st, ch 7 (counts as dc, ch 4), *3 dc in each of next 2 ch-6 loops, ch 4**, 1 dc in next dc, ch 4, rep from * twice, rep from * to ** once, join with a Sl st in 3rd ch of beg ch-7 (8 ch-4 sps).

RND 5: With B, *ch 4, sk next ch-4 sp, Sl st in next dc, ch 10, sk next 4 dc, Sl st in next dc, ch 4, sk next ch-4 sp, Sl st in next dc, rep from * 3 times, ending with last Sl st in same place as first Sl st (4 ch-10 loops, 8 ch-4 sps). Fasten off B.

RND 6: With right side facing, join C in first ch-4 sp, ch 2, 3 hdc in same ch-4 sp, *(5 hdc, ch 3, 5 hdc) in next ch-10 loop**, 4 hdc in each of next ch-4 sps, rep from * twice, rep from * to ** once, 4 hdc in next ch-4 sp, join with a Sl st in 2nd ch of beg ch-2. Fasten off C.

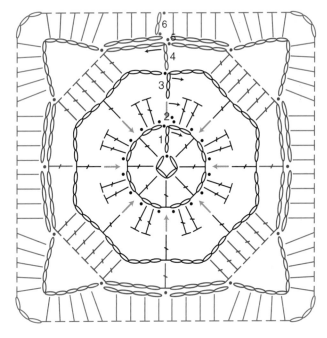

69 | STAR GRASS FLOWER

SKILL LEVEL: Easy

Made with 3 colors: A, B, and C.

Double triple crochet (dtr): Yo (3 times), insert hook in next sp, yo, draw yarn through sp, [yo, draw yarn through 2 loops on hook] 4 times.

With A, ch 6, join with a Sl st to form a ring.

RND 1: With A, ch 3 (counts as dc), 2 dc in ring, ch 3, [3 dc, ch 3] 5 times in ring, Sl st in the 3rd ch of beg ch-3 (6 ch-3 sps). Fasten off A.

RND 2: With right side facing, join B in any ch-3 sp, ch 5, (2 dtr, ch 3, 3 dtr) in same ch-3 sp, (3 dtr, ch 3, 3 dtr) in each ch-3 sp around, join with a Sl st in 5th ch of beg ch-5 (6 ch-3 sps). Fasten off B.

RND 3: With right side facing, join C in any ch-3 sp, ch 3, 2 tr in same sp (half corner made) *ch 2, sk next 3 dtr, 1 dc in sp between last skipped and next dtr, ch 2, sk next 3 dtr, (3 tr, ch 3, 3 tr) in next ch-3 sp (corner made), ch 2, sk next 3 dtr, 1 dc in sp between last skipped and next dtr, ch 2, sk next 3 dtr, 1 sc in next ch-3 sp, ch 2, sk next 3 dtr, 1 dc in sp between last skipped and next dtr, ch 2, sk next 3 dtr*, (3 tr, ch 3, 3 tr) in next ch-3 sp, rep from * to * once, 3 tr in same corner as beg half corner, ch 3, join with a Sl st in 3rd ch of beg ch-3 (completes corner).

RND 4: With C, ch 1, work 1 sc in each st, 2 sc in each ch-2 sp, (2 sc, ch 3, 2 sc) in each corner ch-3 sp around, join with a Sl st in first sc. Fasten off C.

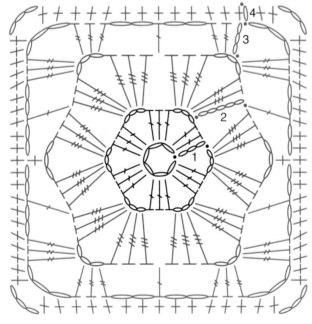

70 | ROSETTA SQUARE

SKILL LEVEL: Intermediate

Made with 2 colors: A and B.

Double triple crochet (dtr): Yo (3 times), insert hook in next sp, yo, draw yarn through sp, [yo, draw yarn through 2 loops on hook] 4 times.

Single crochet 2 together (sc2tog): Insert hook in next st, yo, draw yarn through st, sk next 2 sts, insert hook in next st, yo, draw yarn through st, yo, draw yarn through 3 loops on hook.

With A, ch 8, join with a Sl st to form a ring.

RND 1: With A, 12 sc in ring, join with a Sl st in first sc (12 sc).

RND 2: With A, ch 5 (counts as dc, ch 2), (1 dc, ch 2) in each sc around, join with a Sl st in the 3rd ch of beg ch-5 (12 ch-2 sps).

RND 3: With A, ch 1, 1 sc in same st, *3 sc in the next ch-2 sp**, 1 sc in the next dc, rep from * 10 times, rep from * to ** once, join with a Sl st in first sc (48 sc).

RND 4: With A, ch 5 (counts as dtr), 1 dtr in each of next 3 sc, *ch 6, 1 dtr in each of next 4 sc, rep from *10 times, ch 6, join with a Sl st in 5th ch of the beg ch-5 (12 ch-6 sps).

RND 5: With A, ch 1, sc2tog worked across first 4 dtr, *8 sc in next ch-6 sp**, sc2tog worked across next 4 dtr, rep from * 10 times, rep from * to ** once, join with a Sl st in first st. Fasten off A.

RND 6: With right side facing, join B in top of any sc2tog, ch 4, 1 tr in same st (half corner made), *[ch 2, sk next 3 sc, 1 sc in each of next 2 sc, ch 2, sk next 3 sc, 1 dc in next sc2tog] twice, ch 2, sk next 3 sc, 1 sc in each of next 2 sc, ch 2, sk next 3 sc**, (2 tr, ch 3, 2 tr) in next petal (corner), rep from * twice, rep from * to ** once, join to a Sl st in 4th ch of beg ch-4 (completes corner).

RND 7: With B, ch 1, starting in same st, 1 sc in each of st, 2 sc in each ch-2 sp, (2 sc, ch 3, 2 sc) in each ch-3 corner sp, join with a Sl st to first sc (4 ch-3 sps). Fasten off B.

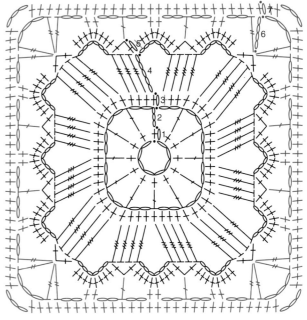

71 | WHIRLPOOL

SKILL LEVEL: Easy

Made with 3 colors: A, B, and C.

With A, ch 6, join with a Sl st to form a ring.

RND 1: With A, ch 6 (counts as dc, ch 3) (1 dc, ch 3) 7 times in ring, join with a Sl st in 3rd ch of beg ch-6 (8 ch-3 sps). Fasten off A.

RND 2: With right side facing, join B in any ch-3 sp, ch 3 (counts as dc here and throughout), 3 dc in same sp, ch 2, (4 dc, ch 2) in each ch-3 sp around, join with a Sl st in 3rd ch of beg ch-3 (8 ch-2 sps). Fasten off B.

RND 3: With right side facing, join C in any ch-2 sp, ch 3, 5 dc in same sp, ch 1, *6 dc, in next ch-2 sp, ch 3** 6 dc in next ch-2 sp, ch 1, rep from * twice, rep from * to ** once, join with a Sl st in 3rd ch of beg ch-3 (8 groups of 6 dc). Fasten off C.

RND 4: With right side facing, join A in any ch-3 sp, ch 3, (1 dc, ch 3, 2 dc) in same sp, *ch 3, 1 sc between the 3rd and 4th dc of next 6-dc group, ch 3, 1 sc in next ch-1 sp, ch 3, 1 sc between 3rd and 4th dc of next 6-dc group, ch 3** (2 dc, ch 3, 2 dc) in next ch-3 sp, rep from * twice, rep from * to ** once, join with a Sl st in 3rd ch of beg ch-3.

RND 5: With A, ch 1, starting in same st, *1 sc in each of next 2 dc, (2 sc, ch 3, 2 sc) in next ch-3 sp, 1 sc in each of next 2 dc, [3 sc in next ch-3 sp, 1 sc in next sc] 3 times, 3 sc in next ch-3 sp, rep from * around, join with a Sl st in first sc. Fasten off.

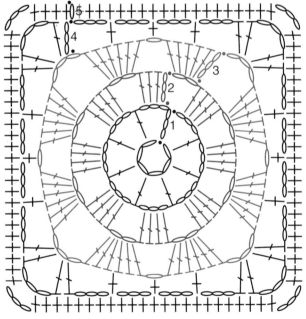

72 | FIESTA

SKILL LEVEL: Intermediate

Made with 5 colors: A, B, C, D, and E.

Popcorn (pc): Work 5 dc in same st or sp, drop loop from hook, insert hook in the first of the 5 dc just made, pick up dropped loop and draw through.

With A ch 4, join with a Sl st to form a ring.

RND 1: With A, ch 4, 3 tr in ring, ch 2, [4 tr, ch 2] 3 times in ring, join with a Sl st in 4th ch of beg ch-4 (4 ch-2 sps). Fasten off A.

RND 2: With right side facing, join B in any ch-2 sp, ch 1, 2 sc in same sp (half corner made), *1 sc in each of next 4 dc**, (2 sc, ch 2, 2 sc) in next ch-2 sp (corner made), rep from * twice, rep from * to ** once, 2 sc in same sp as first half corner, ch 2, join with a Sl st in first sc (4 ch-2 sps). Fasten off B.

RND 3: With right side facing, join C in any corner ch-2 sp, ch 3 (counts as dc here and throughout), 1 dc in same sp (half corner made), *1 dc in each of next 8 sc**, (2 dc, ch 3, 2 dc) in next ch-2 sp (corner made), rep from * twice, rep from * to ** once, 2 dc in same sp as beg half corner, ch 3, join with a Sl st in 3rd ch of beg ch-3 (4 ch-3 sps). Fasten off C.

RND 4: With right side facing, join D in any ch-3 corner sp, ch 3, 2 dc in same sp (half corner made), *ch 2, sk next 2 dc, 1 dc in each of next 8 dc, ch 2, sk next 2 dc**, (3 dc, ch 3, 3 dc) in next ch-3 corner sp (corner made), rep from * twice, rep from * to ** once, 3 dc in same sp as beg half corner, ch 3, join with a Sl st in 3rd ch of beg ch-3 (completes corner) (8 ch-2 sps, 4 ch-3 sps). Fasten off D.

RND 5: With right side facing, join E in any ch-3 corner sp, ch 3, 2 dc in same sp (half corner made), *ch 2, sk next 3 dc, 1 pc in next ch-2 sp, ch 2, sk next 2 dc, 1 dc in each of next 4 dc, ch 2, sk next 2 dc, 1 pc in next ch-2 sp, ch 2, sk next 3 dc**, (3 dc, ch 3, 3 dc) in next ch-3 sp (corner made), rep from * twice, rep from * to ** once, 3 dc, in same sp as first half corner, ch 3, join with a Sl st in 3rd ch of beg ch-3 (completes corner) (32 ch-2 sps, 4 ch-3 sps). Fasten off E.

RND 6: With right side facing, join A in any ch-3 corner sp, ch 1, *(3 sc, ch 2, 3 sc) in ch-3 corner sp (corner made), 1 sc in each of next 3 dc, 2 sc in the next ch-2 sp, 1 sc in next pc, 2 sc in next ch-2 sp, 1 sc in each of next 4 dc, 2 sc in next ch-2 sp, 1 sc in next pc, 2 sc in next ch-2 sp, 1 sc in each of next 3 dc, rep from * 3 times, join with a Sl st in first sc (4 ch-2 sps). Fasten off A.

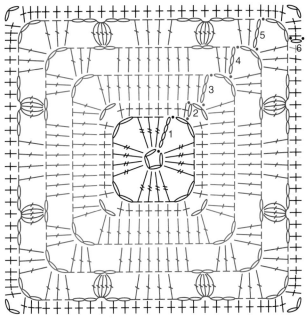

73 | WHIMSY

SKILL LEVEL: Intermediate

Made with 3 colors: A, B, and C.

Triple crochet cluster (tr cluster): [Yo twice, insert hook in next sp, yo, draw yarn through, (yo, draw through 2 loops on hook) twice] twice in same sp, yo, draw yarn through 3 loops on hook.

Double triple crochet (dtr): Yo (3 times), insert hook in next st or sp, yo, draw yarn through, [yo, draw yarn through 2 loops on hook] 4 times.

Double crochet cluster (dc cluster): [Yo, insert hook in next sp, yo, draw yarn through] twice in same sp, yo, draw yarn through 3 loops on hook.

With A, ch 4, join with a Sl st to form a ring.

RND 1: With A, ch 4 (counts as tr), 1 tr in ring (counts as tr cluster), ch 3, [1 tr cluster, ch 3] 7 times in ring, join with a Sl st in first tr (8 clusters, 8 ch-3 sps).

RND 2: With A, Sl st in first ch of the next ch-3 sp, ch 1, (1 sc, ch 5) in center ch of each ch-3 sp around, join with a Sl st in first sc, (8 ch-5 sps). Fasten off A.

RND 3: With right side facing, join B in center ch of any ch-5 sp, ch 1, starting in same sc, *1 sc in in center ch of ch-5 sp, [(1 dtr, ch 1) 10 times, 1 dtr] in next ch-5 sp (fan made), rep from * 3 times, join with a Sl st in first sc (4 fans). Fasten off B.

RND 4: With right side facing, join C in any sc between fans, ch 4 (counts as a tr, ch-1), *(1 dc, ch 1) in each of next 4 ch-1 sps, 1 dc cluster in next ch-1 sp, ch 3 (corner sp made), 1 dc cluster in next ch-1 sp, (1 dc, ch 1) in each of next 4 ch-1 sps**, 1 tr in next sc, ch 1, rep from * twice, rep from * to ** once, join with a Sl st in 3rd ch of beg ch-4 (40 ch-1 sps, 4 ch-3 sps). Fasten off C.

RND 5: With right side facing, join A in any ch-3 corner sp, ch 1, 2 sc in same sp (half corner made), *2 sc in each of next 10 ch-1 sps**, (2 sc, ch 2, 2 sc) in next ch-3 corner sp, rep from * twice, rep from * to ** once, 2 sc in same sp as first half corner, ch 2, join with a Sl st in first sc. Fasten off A.

74 | FLEUR

SKILL LEVEL: Intermediate

Made with 3 colors: A, B, and C.

With A, ch 6, join with a Sl st to form a ring.

RND 1: With A, ch 1, [1 sc, ch 3, tr, ch 3, tr, ch 3] 4 times in ring, join with a Sl st in first sc (4 petals). Fasten off A.

RND 2: With right side facing, join B in last tr made (to the left of any ch-3 sp), ch 1, 1 sc in same tr, *1 sc in top ch of next ch-3 sp, 2 dc in next sc between petals, sc in top ch of next ch-3 sp, 1 sc in next tr, 1 sc in first ch of next ch-3 sp, ch 3, sk next ch, 1 sc in next ch**, 1 sc in next tr, rep from * twice, rep from * to ** once, join with a Sl st in first sc (4 ch-3 sps).

RND 3: With B, ch 3 (counts as dc here and throughout), 1 dc in each of next 6 sc, *(1 dc, ch 3, 1 dc) in next ch-3 sp (corner made)**, 1 dc in each of next 8 sc, rep from * twice, rep from * to ** once, 1 dc in each of the next 2 sc, join with a Sl to in 3rd ch of beg ch-3 (4 ch-3 sps). Fasten off B.

RND 4: With right side facing, join C in any corner ch-3 sp, ch 3, 2 dc in same sp (half corner made), *[ch 2, sk next 2 dc, 1 dc in each of next 2 dc] twice, ch 2, sk next 2 dc**, (3 dc, ch 3, 3 dc) in next ch-3 corner sp (corner made), rep from * twice, rep from * to ** once, 3 dc in same ch-3 sp as first half corner, ch 3, join with a Sl st in 3rd ch of beg ch-3 (completes corner) (12 ch-2 sps, 4 ch-3 sps). Fasten off C.

RND 5: With right side facing, join B in any ch-3 corner sp, ch 3, 2 dc in same sp (half corner made), *1 dc in each of next 3 dc, 2 dc in ch-2 sp, [1 dc in each of next 2 dc, 2 dc in next ch-2 sp] twice, 1 dc in each of next 3 dc**, (3 dc, ch 3, 3 dc) in next ch-3 sp (corner made), rep from * twice, rep from * to ** once, 3 dc in same sp as first half corner, ch 3, join with a Sl st in 3rd ch of beg ch-3 (completes corner). Fasten off.

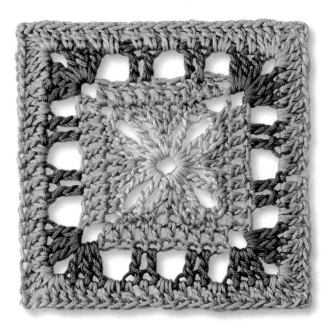

75 | SAVANNAH

SKILL LEVEL: Intermediate

Made with 3 colors: A, B, and C.

With A, ch 3, join with a Sl st to form a ring.

RND 1: With A, ch 3 (counts as dc), 2 dc in ring, ch 2, [3 dc, ch 2] 3 times in ring, join with a Sl st in 3rd ch of beg ch-3 (4 ch-2 sps). Fasten off A.

RND 2: With right side facing, join B in any ch-2 sp, ch 1, 1 sc in same sp, *sk next dc, (3 dc, ch 2, 3 dc) in next dc, sk next dc**, sc in next ch-2 sp, rep from * twice, rep from * to ** once, join with a Sl st in first sc (8 ch-1 sps, 4 ch-2 sps). Fasten off B.

RND 3: With right side facing, join C in any ch-2 sp, ch 1, 1 sc in same sp, *ch 1, (4 dc, ch 2, 4 dc) in next sc, ch 1, sk next 3 dc**, sc in next ch-2 sp, rep from * twice, rep from * to ** once, join with a Sl st in first sc (8 ch-1 sps, 4 ch-2 sps). Fasten off C.

RND 4: With right side facing, join A in any ch-2 corner sp, ch 1, *(1 sc, ch 2, 1 sc) in ch-2 corner sp (corner made), 1 sc in each of next 4 dc, 1 sc in next ch-1 sp, 1 sc in next sc, 1 sc in next ch-1 sp, 1 sc in each of next 4 dc, rep from * 3 times, join with a Sl st in first sc (4 ch-2 sps).

RND 5: Sl st in next ch-2 sp, ch 5, (counts as dc, ch 2), 1 dc in same sp, *1 dc in each of next 13 dc**, (1 dc, ch 2, 1 dc) in next ch-2 sp (corner made), rep from * twice, rep from * to ** once, join with a Sl st in 3rd ch of beg ch-3 (4 ch-2 sps). Fasten off.

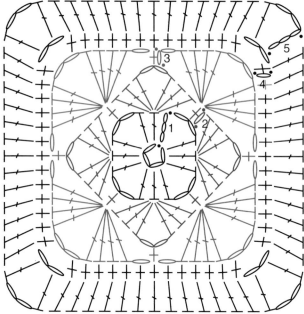

DESIGNING WITH GRANNY SQUARES

Granny squares are versatile building blocks, and the ways to use them are as varied as the people who crochet. Granny square blankets are always popular, and the design choices are endless. But stretch your imagination and you'll easily see how granny squares can be used to design fashion accessories and clothes for everyone in the family.

START SMALL

If you love granny squares and would like a little touch of them, here are some ideas.
All are beginner easy and make great gifts.

HEADBAND OR HATBAND

Make 5 little squares, using a lightweight yarn such as cotton, and a 4/E (3.5 mm) hook, working the first 2 rows of the #4 Classic Granny Square (page 32). Sew together in a strip. Chain 60, join in one corner of strip, work sc along one long end, ch 60, fasten off. Chain 60, join to other corner of strip, work sc along one end, ch 60, fasten off. Join yarn in center sp at one end, ch 60, fasten off. Join yarn in center sp at other end, ch 60, fasten off.

COLLAR BAND

Make eight little squares, using a lightweight yarn such as cotton and a 4/E (3.5 mm) hook, working the first 2 rows of the #4 Classic Granny Square (page 32). Sew together in a strip. Right side facing, join yarn in corner of short end, working in every other st or sp, *sc, ch 3, sc in same st/sp, rep from * along one short end, along one long end, along one short end. Fasten off. Pin on collar, being sure to center at back of neck, allowing picot edge to hang over collar. Sew in place.

MITTEN TOPPERS

Use granny squares to embellish purchased mittens. Using sport weight bamboo yarn and a 4/E (3.5 mm) hook, make two #9 Lilyan's Lace Squares, working only the first three rows, and then fasten off. Center the squares over the button. With yarn and a tapestry needle, work a blanket stitch around each cuff, and then crochet ruffle as follows: *ch 5, sc in next st, rep from * all around cuff, fasten off.

MÖBIUS SCARF

With size 10½/K (6.5 mm) hook, make six #14 Cone Flower Squares (page 45) using Plymouth *Baby Alpaca Grande* for A and *Haciendo* for B. Sew squares together into a long rectangle. Lay scarf flat on surface; flip front to back at one end, and sew to the opposite end. Then apply edging as follows: Row 1: With A, join yarn in any ch-sp, *ch 3, sc in next sp, rep from * all around to where you began, join with a Sl st to the first ch of beg ch-3. Row 2: *1 sc, ch 3, 1 sc in next ch-3 sp, rep from * all around, join with a Sl st to first ch-1, fasten off.

WASHCLOTHS

Choose any square that has a more closed appearance, and crochet it in cotton or linen yarn. Add a few extra rounds until your washcloth is the size you want. Patterns used here are #67 Quartet Squares (page 102) and #10 Great Grandma's Square (page 40).

FELTED COASTERS AND HOT PADS

Crochet any granny square with non-washable wool yarn. Then felt it by washing in hot water in your washing machine. The yarn shrinks and thickens and forms a thick, cushiony fabric that will protect your furniture. These coasters are #61 Isabella Square (page 96). Make them in a larger size to use as hot pads or trivets.

GRAPH IT OUT

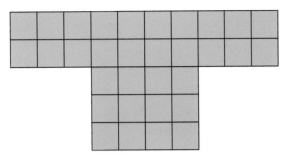

SQUARE-NECK PULLOVER. Leave the top two center squares open for the neck.

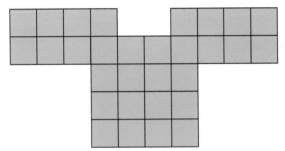

BOAT-NECK PULLOVER. Make the front and back identical or fill in two squares across the back neck.

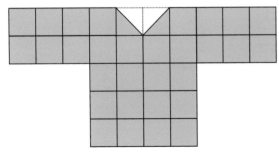

V-NECK PULLOVER. Make half squares for the top center front.

Granny squares are fun to make and are usually one of the first things a crocheter learns to do. Taking the granny square out of the afghan/blanket mode and into fashion requires some ingenuity. Here are some diagrams to show some possibilities for using squares. Many of the garment projects designed for this book began as graphed sketches like these. I am sure that you will come up with more of your own ideas. By studying the illustrations, you will begin to see how to construct a garment from granny squares. The possibilities are endless. Playing with square placement is like working a jigsaw puzzle.

In order to come out with a garment that fits, you have to do some math and some gauge testing. If, for instance, you want a garment to end up being a 40" (101.6 cm) finished width, you would experiment with yarn and hook, and come up with a square that would be about 5" (12.7 cm). Then proceed to make a front and back, each being four squares across, and however many squares long that you want. You also have to use some imagination.

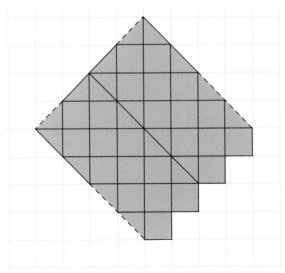

DIAGONAL VEST. Make half squares for the arm openings, neck, and down the front opening. Make full squares that wrap from front to back at the sides and shoulders.

By using half squares, you could make a V-neck shaping, either pullover or V-neck cardigan. If you prefer a more shaped garment, you could work one band of the granny squares using a smaller hook. Another shaping possibility is to work some rows of single crochet at the waistband.

ADDING TO THE SIZE OF A SQUARE

You can change the size of a square quite easily. Let's say you need a square that is 5½" (14 cm), and the square that you love works out to be only 5" (12.7 cm). If working another whole row of the pattern will make the square too large, you can work one row of single crochet all around the outer edge of the square, adding the needed half inch (1.3 cm).

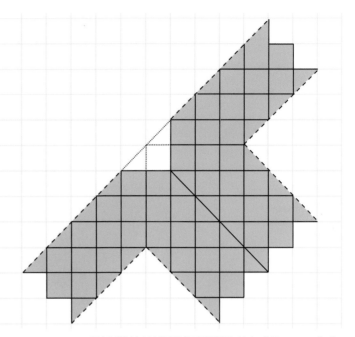

DIAGONAL V-NECK CARDIGAN. Make full squares that wrap from front to back at the sides and sleeves. Half squares for the center fronts and back neck.

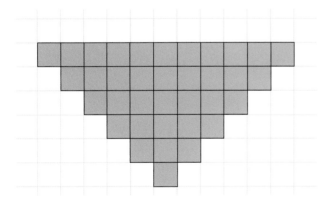

Make a triangle shawl leaving the step edging.

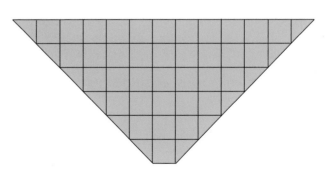

Fill in with half squares along the edges.

The Butterfly Garden Square used for this shaped shawl is an original granny square used with permission from designer Chris Simon. Handpainted cotton yarn has subtle color variations that give the shawl a rich, organic look. I've designed this rectangular shawl with a bit of shaping by sewing shoulder seams and leaving armhole openings. In this configuration, the front edges drape naturally into bias folds, a popular look that can be casual or dressy.

BUTTERFLY GARDEN TWO-WAY SHAWL

SHAPED SHAWL

Make 36 #17 Butterfly Garden Squares (page 48). Arrange squares in a rectangle three squares wide by twelve squares long. Sew squares together with right sides facing, join from back loops of last row (page 25), following the diagram. Note that openings one and three-quarters squares deep are left four squares from each end for armholes. Join edge A to B and C to D to form shoulder seams.

PICOT EDGE

Work picots all around outside edges as follows: Join yarn in any corner st, *ch 3, sk 1 st, 1 sc in next st, rep from * all around, join with a Sl st in base of beg ch-3, fasten off.

Join yarn at underarm seam, work picot edge all around armhole opening. Repeat for other opening.

BLOCKING: Fold vest in half, place on a padded surface, spray with water, pat into shape with fingers, allow to dry.

To simplify the shawl, simply sew the squares together into a rectangle and add picot edging at the ends.

YARN Blue Heron Yarns 100% Egyptian mercerized cotton, 8 oz (227 g)/1000 yd (914.5 m): raspberry, 2 skeins

HOOK 6/G (4 mm)

GAUGE 1 square = 6" x 6" (15 x 15 cm)

NOTIONS tapestry needle

FINISHED SIZE 18" x 72" (45.5 x 183 cm)

SKILL LEVEL Intermediate

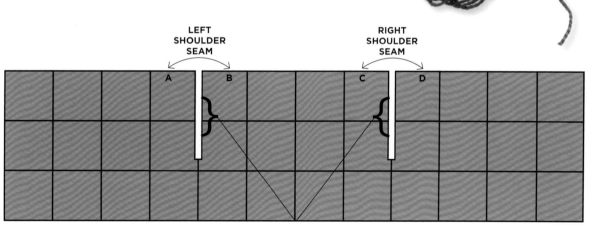

LEFT SHOULDER SEAM

RIGHT SHOULDER SEAM

A   B   C   D

LEAVE OPEN FOR ARMHOLE

Granny square lace? Absolutely! This lovely cashmere and silk lace-weight yarn works up beautifully following the directions for the Popcorns and Lace Square. Finishing this shawl is a breeze, too, because you simply stitch the squares together in a long V shape. I added a scalloped edging to finish it off. Light as a feather and warm as a hug, this shawl is truly a dream to wear.

POPCORNS AND LACE SHAWL

SHAWL

Make 20 #55 Popcorns and Lace Squares (page 90).

Assemble the squares following the diagram, using the single crochet seam, page 26.

EDGING

*Triple crochet 3 together (tr3tog): *Yo twice, pick up a loop in designated stitch, [yo, draw through 2 loops on hook] twice, rep from * twice in same stitch, yo, draw through all 4 loops on hook.*

Work Three Petal Scallop on outside edges as follows:

ROW 1: Working from RS, join yarn in bottom left corner ch-3 sp of scarf, * ch 8, Sl st in fourth ch from hook (picot made), ch 4, sk next 3 dc and 1 ch-1 sp, 1 sc in next ch-1 sp, ch 8, Sl st in fourth ch from hook (picot made), sk next 3 ch-1 sps, 1 sc in next dc, ch 8, Sl st in fourth ch from hook (picot made), ch 4, sk next 3 ch-1 sps, sc in next sp, ch 8, Sl st in fourth ch from hook (picot made), ch 4, 1 sc in corner sp, 1 sc in corner sp of next square. Repeat from * around outer edge of shawl, turn.

ROW 2: Ch 4, *[tr3tog, ch 5, tr3tog, ch 5, tr3tog] in next picot, 1 tr in next sc, rep from * around, ch 4, join with Sl st to beginning corner sp, fasten off.

If blocking is needed, lay on a padded surface, spray lightly with water, pat into shape, allow to dry.

YARN Filatura DiCrosa *Superior*, 70% cashmere, 30% Schappe silk, 0.88 oz (25 g)/330 yd (300 m): #19, 3 balls

HOOK 6/G (4 mm)

GAUGE 1 square = 6" x 6" (15 x 15 cm)

NOTIONS Tapestry needle

FINISHED SIZE 13" x 38" (33 x 96.5 cm)

SKILL LEVEL Experienced

Choose yarn with a little sparkle woven through its fibers to give your project holiday glitz. This vest goes together quickly using the Dogwood Flower Square motif. This cropped length wears well over a long-tail shirt or a tucked-in top and belted jeans. If you prefer a longer length, add more rows of squares.

HOLIDAY VEST

Same number of squares made for each size; width and length are changed by adding dc rows to sides and bottom.

MAIN BODY

Make 40 #11 Dogwood Flower Squares (page 42).

Make 2 half squares as follows:

Half squares are made in rows, not rounds.

FOUNDATION: Ch 10, join with a Sl st to form a ring.

ROW 1: Ch 3, 4 dc in ring, ch 7, 5 dc in ring, turn.

ROW 2: Ch 6, 2 dc in 3rd ch, ch 2, 1 dc in each of next 2 dc, 2 dc in next dc, 1 dc in each of next 2 dc, (3 dc, ch 5, 3 dc) in ch-7 sp, 1 dc in each of next 2 dc, 2 dc in next dc, 1 dc in each of next 2 dc, ch 2, 3 dc in 3rd ch of beg ch-3, turn.

ROW 3: Ch 6 (counts as 1 dc, ch 3), sk 1 dc, 1 dc in next dc, ch 5, sk 1 dc, cluster (same as cluster in main square) in next 6 dc, ch 5, sk 1 dc, 1 dc in next dc, ch 3, sk 1 dc (2 dc, ch 3, 2 dc) in next ch-5 sp, ch 3, sk 1 dc, 1 dc in next dc, ch 5, sk 1 dc, cluster in next 6 dc, ch 5, sk 1 dc, 1 dc in next dc, ch 3, sk 1 dc, 1 dc in tch, turn.

ROW 4: Ch 1, *[3 sc in next ch space] twice, 1 sc in top of cluster, rep between [ ] twice*, 1 sc in ea of next 2 dc, 3 sc in next ch-3 sp, 1 sc in ea of next 2 dc, rep from * to * once, end 1 sc in 3rd ch of beg ch-6, fasten off.

Sew squares right sides together from back loop.

For size Small assemble body as shown in diagram (page 126).

For size Medium add 1 row of dc on each side of the underarm squares before seaming.

For size Large add 2 rows of dc on each side of the underarm squares before seaming.

Sew shoulders and underarm seams.

BOTTOM BORDER

Begin at bottom right front, right side facing you:

ROW 1: Work in sc, picking up 23 sc in each square and each half square all around to bottom left front, turn.

ROW 2: Ch 1, 1 sc in each sc to bottom right front, turn.

ROW 3: (Buttonhole row) Mark 7 buttonholes using bottom and center of squares as placement points, starting at bottom and ending at V-neck shaping, *work sc to marker, ch 2, sk 2 chains, rep from * 6 times more, cont in sc to bottom left front, turn.

(continued)

YARN Lion Brand *Vanna's Glamour*, 96% acrylic, 4% metallic polyester, 1.75 oz (50 g)/202 yd (185 m): jewel #146, 4, (4, 5) skeins

HOOK 6/G (4 mm)

GAUGE 1 square = 3½" x 3½" (9 x 9 cm)

FINISHED SIZE Small (Medium, Large) Finished chest size 36" (38", 40") (91.5 [96.5, 101.5] cm)

SKILL LEVEL Intermediate

ROW 4: 1 sc in each sc, 2 sc in ea ch-2 sp to bottom of right front, turn.

ROW 5: 1 sc in each sc, do not turn.

ROW 6: Work 1 row of reverse sc, fasten off.

ARMHOLE BORDER

RND 1: Join at underarm, work 1 row sc as follows, * 1 sc in each of next 2 sts, sk 1 st, repeat from * around, join with a Sl st, do not turn.

RND 2: *1 sc in in each of next 14 sc, sk 1 st, rep from * around, join with a Sl st.

RND 3: 1 sc in each st around.

RND 4: Reverse sc in each st around.

If blocking is needed, lay garment on a padded surface, spray with water, pat gently into shape, allow to dry.

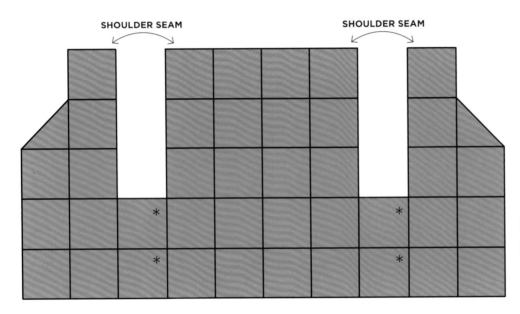

SHOULDER SEAM   SHOULDER SEAM

*ADD STITCHES TO SIDES OF THESE SQUARES BEFORE ASSEMBLY FOR MEDIUM AND LARGE SIZES.

YOGA TUNIC AND MAT CARRIER

DESIGNED BY SHARON VALENCIA

Cool turquoise is a relaxing color, perfect for this yoga tunic designed by my daughter. The Yoga Tunic is worked in an unusual manner, first making the motifs, then working from side to side, creating the flattering vertical lines of the pattern. This project is a little challenging but rewarding as there is very little finishing work to do. And even if you're not the most flexible student in the yoga class, you will be the most stylish when you transport your mat in this handy carrier. Easy to crochet and even easier to use, the carrier simply rolls around your mat and buttons in place above a row of colorful granny squares. Sling into the shoulder strap and you're ready to go.

TUNIC

GRANNY SQUARE BAND

Make 17 #28 Paula's Pendant Squares (page 61), working first 6 rnds only, working 1 rnd each of A, B, C, and D, and 2 rnds of E.

Sew squares in a strip, as shown below.

ROW 1: With right side facing, join E in lower left corner space of first square, ch 2 (counts as dc), *work 1 dc in each st along edge of square, dc in next corner sp**, dc in corner sp of next square, rep from * across, ending last rep at **, turn (18 dc across each square side; 306 dc).

(continued)

YARN For Tunic: Tahki *Cotton Classic*, 100% mercerized cotton, 1.75 oz (50 g), 108 yd (100 m): aqua #3777 (E), 14 skeins; and 2 skeins each canteloupe #3476 (A); bright lime green #3726 (B); light raspberry #3457 (C); and bright blue #3806 (D).

For Mat Carrier: bright lime green #3806 (B), 2 skeins; small amounts of colors A, C, D, and E, left over from Tunic. If you are making the Mat Carrier alone, you will need 1 skein each of colors A, C, D, and E.

HOOK F/5 (3.75 mm)

GAUGE 1 square =
4¼" x 4¼" (11 x 11 cm)

17 dc = 4¼" (11 cm)

8 rows = 4" (10 cm)

NOTIONS

for Tunic: five ¾" (2 cm) buttons

for Mat Carrier: tapestry needle
six ⅝" (1.5 cm) buttons
sewing needle and thread

FINISHED SIZE

Tunic: finished bust: 42" (106.5 cm)

46" (117 cm) at bottom edge

19" (48.5 cm) long from underarm

If larger size is desired use 6/G (4 mm) hook. This will result in a wider, longer tunic.

Mat Carrier: 13" x 17½" (33 x 44.5 cm)

SKILL LEVEL Experienced

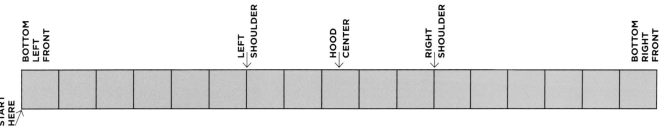

BOTTOM LEFT FRONT   LEFT SHOULDER   HOOD CENTER   RIGHT SHOULDER   BOTTOM RIGHT FRONT

START HERE

Cotton yarn is a classic choice for a tunic that is both functional and pretty. Comfortable and cool, this button-front jacket is easy-wear and easy-care.

RIGHT FRONT

ROW 2: Ch 2 (counts as a dc here and throughout), sk first dc, 1 dc in each of the next 107 dc, for a total of 108 dc. This brings you to the top edge of the 6th square (top of right shoulder seam, see diagram, page 127), turn, leaving remaining sts unworked.

ROW 3: Ch 1, 1 sc in each of first 36 dc, 1 dc in each of next 72 dc, turn. Note: This brings you to the bottom right front of the sweater. (See diagram, page 127.)

ROWS 4-9: Rep rows 2 and 3 (3 times).

ARMHOLE SHAPING:

ROW 10: Ch 2, 1 dc in each of next 71 sts, 1 sc in each of next 18 sts, turn, leaving remaining sts unworked.

ROW 11: Ch 1, 1 sc in each of next 18 sc, 1 dc in each of next 72 dc, turn (90 sts).

ROW 12: Ch 2, 1 dc in each of next 71 dc, 1 sc in each of next 9 sc, turn, leaving remaining sts unworked (81 sts).

ROW 13: Ch 1, 1 sc in each of next 9 sc, 1 dc in each of next 72 dc, turn. (Beginning of row 13 is bottom of underarm.)

ROW 14: Ch 2, 1 dc in each of next 71 dc, ch 10, turn.

ROW 15: Beg in 2nd ch from hook, 1 sc in next 9 ch, 1 dc in each of next 72 dc, turn (81 sts).

ROW 16: Ch 2, 1 dc in each of next 71 dc, 1 sc in each of next 9 sc, ch 10, turn.

ROW 17: Beg in 2nd ch from hook, 1 sc in each of next 9 ch, 1 sc in each of next 9 sts, 1 dc in each of next 72 dc, turn (90 sts).

ROW 18: Ch 2, 1 dc in each of next 71 dc, 1 sc in each of next 18 sc, ch 19, turn.

ROW 19: Beg in 2nd ch from hook, work 1 sc in each of next 18 ch, 1 sc in each of next 18 sts, 1 dc in each of next 72 dc, turn (108 sts). (Armhole shaping complete. See diagram, page 130.)

ROW 20: Ch 2, 1 dc in each of next 107 dc, turn (108 dc).

ROW 21: Ch 1, 1 sc in each of next 36 sc, 1 dc in each of next 72 dc, turn.

ROWS 22-27: Rep rows 20 and 21 (3 times).

ROW 28: Fold sweater at underarm "seam" (at bottom of armhole shaping), ch 2, 1 dc in each of next 107 sts, (108 dc). Starting in edges of next square above right front, where you left off on row 2, work 18 dc across each of next 2 squares, work 9 dc across to center of next square, ch 2, turn, leaving remaining sts of square unworked.

ROWS 29-36: Ch 2, 1 dc in each of next 152 sts (153 sts). Note: You should be at the top center back of sweater. Fasten off, leaving a strand long enough to sew top seam of hood.

LEFT FRONT

ROW 1: With wrong side facing, join E at left shoulder edge, at the top of the 6th square above opposite end of assembled squares. Ch 1, starting in same st, 1 sc in each of next 36 sts, 1 dc in each of the next 72 dc, turn (108 sts).

ROW 2: Ch 2, 1 dc in each st across, turn.

ROW 3: Ch 1, 1 dc in each of next 72 dc, 1 sc in each of next 36 sc, turn.

ROWS 4-9: Rep rows 2 and 3 (3 times).

ARMHOLE SHAPING:

ROW 10: Ch 2, 1 dc in each of next 71 sts, 1 sc in each of next 18 sc, turn, leaving remaining sts unworked (90 sts).

ROW 11: Ch 1, sc in each of first 18 sc, dc in each st across, turn.

ROW 12: Ch 2, 1 dc in each of next 71 dc, 1 sc in each of next 9 sc, turn, leaving remaining sts unworked (81 sts).

ROW 13: Ch 1, 1 sc in each of next 9 sc, 1 dc in each of next 72 dc, turn. (Beginning of row 13 is bottom of underarm.)

ROW 14: Ch 2, 1 dc in each of next 71 dc, ch 10, turn, leaving remaining sts unworked.

ROW 15: Beg in the 2nd ch from hook, 1 sc in each of next 9 sc, 1 dc in each of next 72 dc, turn (81 sts).

ROW 16: Ch 2, 1 dc in each of next 71 sts, 1 sc in each of next 9 sc, ch 10, turn.

ROW 17: Beg in 2nd ch from hook, 1 sc in each of next 9 ch, 1 sc in each of next 9 sts, 1 dc in each of next 72 dc, turn (90 sts). Ch 2, 1 dc in each of next 71 dc, 1 dc in each of next 18 sc, ch 19, turn.

ROW 18: Beg in 2nd ch from hook, 1 sc in each of next 18 ch, 1 sc in each of next 18 sts, 1 dc in each of next 72 dc, turn (108 sts). (Armhole shaping complete)

ROW 19: Ch 2, 1 dc in each of next 107 dc, turn.

ROW 20: Ch 1, 1 sc in each of next 36 sts, 1 dc in each of next 72 dc, turn.

ROWS 21-26: Rep rows 19 and 20 (3 times).

(continued)

ROW 27: Ch 2, 1 dc in each of next 107 dc. Fasten off, leaving a strand long enough to sew shoulder seam. Sew shoulder seam from wrong side of work.

ROW 28: With wrong side facing, join E with a Sl st to center back of hood (see fig 2), ch 2, work 8 dc along remaining half square, 18 dc across each of next 2 squares (45 dc in all), dc in each st across row 27, turn (153 dc).

ROWS 29–36: Ch 2, 1 dc in each of the next 152 sts, turn, ending last row at bottom center back of sweater. Fasten off leaving a strand long enough to sew center back seam.

SLEEVES

Starting at underarm seam, ch 54.

ROW 1: Starting in 2nd ch from hook, 1 dc in each ch across, ch 11, turn (53 dc).

ROW 2 (begin cap shaping): Beg in 2nd ch from hook, work 1 sc in each of next 10 ch, 1 sc in each of next 2 dc, 1 dc in each dc across, turn (63 sts).

ROW 3: ch 2, 1 dc in each of next 50 dc, 1 sc in each of next 12 sc, ch 11, turn.

ROW 4: Starting in 2nd ch from hook, 1 sc in each next 10 ch, 1 sc in each of next 12 sc, 1 dc in each dc across, turn (73 sts).

ROW 5: Ch 2, 1 dc in each of next 50 dc, 1 dc in each st across to last 2 sts, 2 dc in next sc (inc made), 1 dc in next sc, turn (74 sts).

ROW 6: Ch 2, 2 dc in next dc (inc made), 1 dc in each dc across, turn (75 dc).

ROWS 7–12: Rep row 5 and 6 (3 times) (81 sts at end of last row).

ROW 13: Ch 2, 1 dc in each of next 50 dc, 1 sc in each of next 30 dc, turn.

ROWS 14–16: Ch 2, 1 dc in each st across, turn.

ROW 17: Rep row 13.

ROW 18: Ch 2, dc2tog over next 2 sts (dec made), dc in each st across, turn (80 dc).

ROW 19: Ch 2, dc in each st across to last 3 sts, dc2tog over next 2 sts (dec made), 1 dc in tch, turn (79 dc).

ROWS 20–25: Rep rows 18 and 19 (3 times) (73 dc at end of last row).

ROW 26: Ch 1, 1 sc in each of next 20 dc, 1 dc in each st across (73 sts), turn.

ROW 27: Ch 2, 1 dc in each of next 50 dc, 1 sc in each of the next 12 sts, turn, leaving remaining 10 sts unworked.

ROW 28: Ch 1, 1 sc in each of the next 12 sc, 1 dc in each st across, turn (63 sts).

ROW 29: Ch 2, 1 dc in each of the next 52 sts, leaving remaining 10 sts unworked. Fasten off.

FINISHING

With E, sew right side shoulder, center back, and center top of hood. Sew underarm sleeve seam. Mark center of sleeve cap, pin in place matching underarm seam, matching center of cap with shoulder seam, sew in place.

HOOD CENTER

RIGHT SHOULDER SEAM

LEFT SHOULDER SEAM

FOLD

FOLD

FRONT AND HOOD BORDER

ROW 1: With right side facing, join E at bottom right corner, ch 1, sc evenly across working 18 sc across each square, turn (306 sc).

ROW 2: Ch 1, 1 sc in each of the next 216 sc, ending at the end of the 12th square, *ch 2, sk 2 sc (buttonhole made), 1 sc in each of the next 7 sc, rep from * 4 times, (5 buttonholes made), 1 sc in each sc across, turn.

ROW 3: Ch 1, *1 sc in each st to next ch-2 sp, 2 sc in next ch-2 sp, rep from * 4 times, 1 sc in each sc across to bottom edge. Fasten off.

Sew buttons to left front edge, opposite buttonholes.

BLOCKING: Place garment on a padded surface, sprinkle with water, pat into place, allow to dry. Ironing is not recommended.

MAT CARRIER

SQUARES

Make 3 #28 Paula's Pendant Squares (page 61), working first 6 rows only, following colors as for the tunic (page 127).

Sew sides together to form a row of 3 squares.

When 3 squares are sewn together, with E, work 1 row sc all around outside edges.

MAIN BODY

ROW 1: With right side facing you, join B in first corner, ch 2 (counts as dc), *1 sc in each of next 17 dc, 1 sc in corner, rep from * twice more, end last dc in last corner (54 dc), turn.

ROW 2 (buttonhole row): Ch 1, 1 sc in first dc, ch 1, sk 2 dc, *1 sc in each of next 8 dc, ch 1, sk 2 dc, rep from * 4 times more, end 1 sc in the 3rd ch of the beg ch-3, (six ch-1 sps for buttonholes) turn.

ROW 3: Ch 2 (counts as dc) sk first sc, 2 dc in the next ch-1 sp, *1 dc in each of the next 8 sc, 2 dc in next ch-1 sp, rep from * 4 times more, end 1 dc in the last sc, turn.

ROWS 4-29: Ch 2 (counts as dc), sk first dc, 1 dc in each of next 52 dc, 1 dc in the turning ch. Fasten off after row 29.

STRAP

FOUNDATION ROW: With B, ch 12, starting in 3rd ch from hook, work 1 dc in each ch (10 dc), turn.

ROWS 1-67: Ch 2 (counts as dc), sk first dc, 1 dc in each of next 8 dc, 1 dc in tch, turn.

FINISHING

With right side facing, sew short ends of strap to sides of main body at opposite end of motifs. Sew buttons along the same edge as straps.

Blocking not necessary.

If you know me, you know I love flowers. I designed this cardigan using eighty #54 Popcorn Squares, with some slight adjustments. This cotton yarn comes in many beautiful colors, so I chose a handful of cheerful brights for the popcorn flowers and a rich, deep orchid for the background. I love how the flowers seem to be floating on top of the fabric.

POPCORN FLOWER CARDIGAN

Beginning popcorn (beg pc): Ch 2, work 4 hdc in designated st, remove hook from last loop, place hook from front to back in top of the first of last 5 dc, pick up dropped loop, draw through loop on hook to complete pc.

Popcorn (pc): Work 5 hdc in designated st, remove hook from last loop, place hook from front to back in top of the first of last 5 dc, pick up dropped loop, draw through loop on hook to complete pc.

Single crochet 2 together (sc2tog): [Insert hook in next st, yo, draw yarn through st] twice, yo, draw yarn through 3 loops on hook.

Reverse single crochet (rev sc): Working from left to right, insert hook in next st to the right, yo, draw yarn through st, yo, draw yarn through 2 loops on hook.

MOTIFS

Using D/3 (3.25 mm) hook, make 80 #54 Popcorn Squares (page 89), 20 each using A, B, C, and D for contrasting center color (CC). Always use MC for rounds 3, 4, and 5.

With CC, ch 8, join with a Sl st to form a ring.

RND 1: With CC, ch 1, work 16 sc in ring, join with a Sl st to first sc (16 sc).

RND 2: Beg pc in first sc, ch 3, *pc in next sc, ch 3, sk next sc, rep from * 6 times, join with a Sl st in beg pc (8 pc, 8 ch-3 sps). Fasten off CC.

RND 3: With right side facing, join MC in any pc, ch 1, sc in same st, *ch 4, 1 sc in top of next pc**, ch 6, 1 sc in top of next pc, rep from * twice, rep from * to ** once, ch 3, dc in first sc (counts as last ch-6 sp) (4 ch-4 sps, 4 ch-6 sps).

RND 4: Ch 2 (counts as hdc), 4 hdc in same sp (half corner), *ch 3, 1 sc in next ch-4 sp, ch 3**, (5 hdc, ch 3, 5 hdc) in next ch-6 sp (corner), rep from * twice, rep from * to ** once, 5 hdc in the same sp as beg half corner, ch 3, join with a Sl st to 2nd ch of beg ch-2 (completes corner).

RND 5: Ch 5 (counts as hdc, ch 3), *1 sc in next ch-3 sp, ch 3, 1 sc in next ch-3 sp, ch 4**, (5 hdc, ch 3, 5 hdc) in next ch-3 sp (corner), ch 3, rep from * twice, rep from * to ** once, (5 hdc, ch 3, 4 hdc) in next ch 3 sp, join with a Sl st to 2nd ch of beg ch-5 (completes corner). Fasten off.

(continued)

YARN Patons Grace, 100% mercerized cotton, 1.75 oz (50 g)/136 yd (125 m): orchid #62307 (MC), 12 (13, 14) skeins; 1 skein each (for all sizes) ginger #62027 (A), azure #62104 (B), lemon lime #62222 (C), viola #62322 (D)

HOOKS C/2 (2.75 mm) and D/3 (3.25 mm)

GAUGE 1 square = 3" x 3" (7.5 x 7.5 cm) with D/3 (3.25 mm) hook

20 dc = 4" (10 cm)

4 rows dc = 1½" (4 cm)

NOTIONS Tapestry needle

seven ¾" (2 cm) buttons

sewing needle and matching thread

FINISHED SIZE
Small (Medium, Large)

Finished bust: 43" (44½", 46") (109 [113, 117] cm)

SKILL LEVEL Experienced

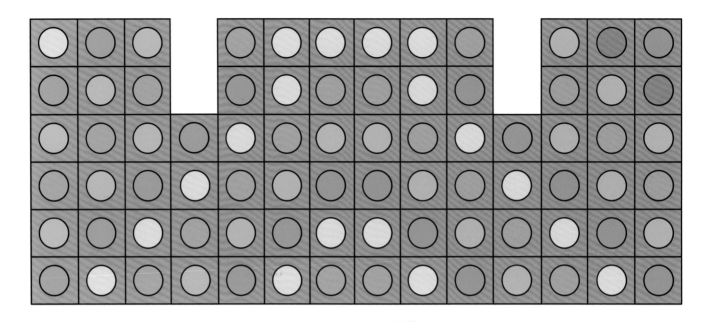

JOINING MOTIFS

SIZE MEDIUM: Before joining, add 1 row of dc along vertical edges of 8 underarm squares.

SIZE LARGE: Before joining, add 2 rows of dc along vertical edges of 8 underarm squares.

ALL SIZES: Join motifs together following diagram above as follows:

JOINING ROW: With right sides together, working through double thickness of 2 motifs, join MC with sc in both corner sps, ch 3, sc in both center hdc of next 5-hdc group, ch 2. (sc, ch 2) in each of next 3 ch-3 sps, sc in center hdc of next 5-hdc group, ch 3, sc in both corner sps. Repeat joining row joining all motifs. For Medium and Large side motifs, join adjacent motifs to corresponding dcs on sides of underarm motifs to join.

When all motifs are joined as per assembly diagram, shape shoulders as follows:

BACK RIGHT SHOULDER:

ROW 1: With right side facing, join MC in top right corner of back, work 24 dc evenly between corner sts of first motif and center of next motif, turn (25 dc).

ROW 2: Ch 3, dc2tog over next 2 sts, dc in each st across, turn (24 dc).

ROW 3: Ch 3, dc in each dc across (24 dc), turn. Fasten off size Small.

SIZES MEDIUM AND LARGE ONLY:

ROWS 4–5 (4–7): Rep row 3. Fasten off.

BACK LEFT SHOULDER:

ROW 1: Sk center 2 motifs on back, join MC in center of next motif (1½ motifs from end), ch 3, work 24 dc evenly spd across to top left-hand corner of back, turn.

ROW 2: Ch 3, dc in next 22 dc, dc2tog over last 2 sts, turn.

ROW 3: Ch 3, dc in each dc across. Fasten off size Small.

SIZES MEDIUM AND LARGE ONLY:

ROWS 4–5 (4–7): Rep row 3. Fasten off.

Work front shoulders to correspond. Sew shoulder seams together.

KEY

= A
= B
= C
= D

*ADD STITCHES TO SIDES OF THESE SQUARES BEFORE ASSEMBLY FOR MEDIUM AND LARGE SIZES.

BOTTOM BORDER

SIZE SMALL ONLY:

ROW 1: With right side facing, and D/3 (3.25 mm) hook, join MC in bottom left-hand corner sp, *ch 3 in corner sp (counts as dc), 1 dc in first, 3rd and 5th hdc of next 5-hdc group, 2 dc in next ch-sp, 1 dc in next sc, 1 dc in next ch-sp, 1 dc in next sc, 2 dc in next ch-sp, 1 dc in first, 3rd and 5th hdc of next 5-hdc group**, 1 dc in corner sp, 1 dc in junction between motifs, rep from * across, ending last rep at **, dc in 2nd ch of last ch-3 sp, turn (15 dc per motif block, plus 1 dc in each junction—223 dc).

SIZES MEDIUM AND LARGE ONLY:

Work same as size Small row 1, working 2 dc in each row-end dc on each added row on side motifs (231 [239] dc).

ALL SIZES:

ROW 2: Ch 4 (counts as dc, ch 1), sk next st, *dc in next st, ch 1, sk next st, rep from * to last st, dc in last st, turn.

ROW 3: Ch 3, dc in each st and ch-1 sp across. Do not fasten off. Rotate piece to work across right front edge.

FRONT AND NECKLINE BORDER

ROW 1: With C/2 hook, ch 1, work 3 sc across edge of bottom border, work 15 sc across each motif to neck edge, work 3 sc in corner sp, work 20 (22, 24) sc evenly spaced to shoulder seam, work 36 (40, 42) sc evenly spaced across back of neck to shoulder, work 20 (22, 24) sc across to top of left front, work 3 sc in corner sp, work 15 sc across each motif of left front edge, work 3 sc across bottom border, turn (268 [276, 284] sc).

ROW 2: Ch 1, sc in each st to corner, 3 sc in center corner sc, sk next sc, sc in each next 16 sc, sc2tog over next 2 sts, sc in each sc to shoulder seam, working along back of neck, *sc in next 4 (6, 4) sc, sc2tog over next 2 sts, rep from * across back of neck to shoulder seam, sc2tog over next 2 sts, sc in next 16 sc, sc2tog over next 2 sts, sc in each sc to corner sc, 3 sc in corner sc, sc in each sc across right front edge to bottom corner, turn.

ROW 3: Ch 1, 1 sc in each next 2 sts, *ch 3, sk next 2 sts (buttonhole made)**, sc in next 13 sts, rep from * 5 times, rep from * to ** once, sc in each sc to corner sc, 3 sc in corner sc, sk next sc, sc in each sc across to first sc before next corner sc, sk next sc, 3 sc in corner sc, sk next sc, sc in each sc across left front edge, turn.

ROW 4: Ch 1, sc in each sc to corner sc, 3 sc in corner sc, sk next sc, sc in each sc across to first sc before next corner sc, sk next sc, 3 sc in corner sc, *sc in each sc to next ch 3 sp, 2 sc in ch-3 sp, rep from * across, sc in last 2 sts, ch 1, turn.

ROW 5: Sc in each sc to center corner st, 3 sc in corner sc, sk next sc, sc in each sc across to first sc before next corner sc, sk next sc, 3 sc in corner sc, sc in each sc across to end, do not turn.

ROW 6: Working from left to right, ch 1, rev sc in each st across right front, neck, and left front edges. Fasten off.

BOTTOM EDGING:

ROW 1: With C/2 (2.75 mm) hook, join MC in bottom left-hand corner, ch 1, sc in each st across bottom edge. Fasten off.

SLEEVE (MAKE 2)

With MC and C/2 (2.75 mm) hook, ch 61.

ROW 1: Working in back loops of ch sts, sc in 2nd ch from hook and in each ch across, turn (60 sc).

ROWS 2 AND 3: Ch 1, sc in each sc across, turn.

ROW 4: Change to D/3 (3.25 mm) hook, ch 1, dc in each sc across, turn.

Continue working in dc, inc 1 dc on each side of every 4th (3rd, 3rd) row, 10 (12, 14) times (80 [84, 88] dc). Work even in dc until sleeve measures 16½" (17", 17½") (42 [43, 44.5] cm) from beg. Fasten off. Sew sleeve seam.

SLEEVE EDGING:

ROW 1: With right side facing, and D/3 (3.25 mm) hook, working across opposite side of foundation ch, join MC at sleeve seam, ch 3 (counts as dc), dc in each ch around, join with a Sl st in 3rd ch of beg ch-3.

ROW 2: Ch 4, sk next st, *dc in next st, ch 1, sk next st, rep from * around, join with a Sl st in 3rd ch of beg ch-4.

ROW 3: Ch 3, dc in each st and ch-1 sp around, join with a Sl st in 3rd ch of beg ch-3.

ROW 4: Ch 1, sc in each st around, join with a Sl st in first sc.

ROW 5: Ch 1, working from left to right, reverse sc in each sc around, join with a Sl st in first reverse sc. Fasten off.

FINISHING

Pin sleeves in place and sew into armholes.

Sew buttons to left front opposite buttonholes.

If blocking is necessary, lay garment on a padded surface, spray lightly with water. Pat into shape and allow to dry. Do not press with iron as this will ruin texture of flowers.

Here's a fun, colorful bag to brighten up any outfit. I'm a big fan of this cotton yarn because it is so easy to work with and it comes in so many vivid colors. Try different combinations of three colors to see what you like. A fabric lining peeks through the holes in the squares and keeps small items from dropping through.

FIESTA BAG

SQUARES

Make 20 #64 Erica Squares (page 99) in color sequence as follows:

4 solid A

4 solid B

4 solid C

2 using A as color 1, C as color 2, B as color 3, A as color 4

2 using B as color 1, C as color 2, B as color 3, A as color 4

4 using C as color 1, A as color 2, B as color 3, A as color 4

Sew squares together following diagram.

SIDE EDGING

Using B, working along short sides, work 2 rows of dc on each side, picking up 20 dc along each square.

Block piece by laying on a flat surface, spray with water, pat into shape, allow to dry.

FINISHING

When dry, cut lining at least 1" (2.5 cm) bigger than piece, pin in place folding edges ½" (1.3 cm) under, sew in place. Fold bag in half, sew side seams one and one half squares, leaving one half square at top open.

TOP BORDER

ROW 1: With B, join in top corner, work 1 dc in every other st along top, ch 1, turn.

ROW 2: Work 1 sc in every other dc, fasten off, leaving a 2 yd (1.85 m) end for sewing to handle.

Rep rows 1 and 2 on other side.

Thread the 2 yd (1.85 m) of yarn onto a tapestry needle and working around the handle, attach handle to last row of sc, fasten off securely.

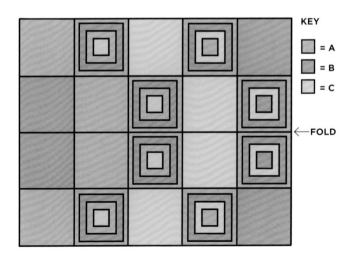

YARN Tahki *Cotton Classic*, 100% mercerized cotton, 1.75 oz (50 g)/108 yd (100 m): 2 skeins each purple #3932 (A), rose #3457 (B), orange #3473 (C).

HOOK 5/F (3.75 mm)

GAUGE 1 square = 3¾" x 3¾" (9.5 x 9.5 cm)

NOTIONS Wooden handles (I used Accessories Unlimited Wooden Handle # 05203, 7.5" x 5" (19 x 12.7 cm)

¾ yd (68.6 cm) of lining fabric

SKILL LEVEL Intermediate

KEY

◻ = A

◻ = B

◻ = C

←FOLD

These earrings are crocheted using super fine metallic braid, following the directions for the #68 Gracie Square with some changes. By eliminating some of the chains between groups the square becomes a little smaller and the center pops a little to give them dimension.

PENDANT EARRINGS

First 3 rounds of this pattern are worked from the wrong side.

FOUNDATION: With A, ch 4, join with a Sl st to form a ring.

RND 1 (WS): With A, ch 5, * 1 dc in ring, ch 2, rep from * 6 times more, join with a Sl st to 3rd ch of beg ch-5 (8 ch-2 sps).

RND 2: With A: *Sl st into next ch-2 sp, 2 dc, 1 Sl st in same sp, rep from * 7 times more, 1 Sl st into same place as first Sl st.

RND 3: With A: ch 6 *1 dc between the two Sl sts, ch 4, rep from *6 times more, join with a Sl st into 3rd ch of beg ch-6, pick up a loop with B, fasten off A, turn work around.

RND 4 (RS): With B, ch 6, *3 dc into each of the next two ch-4 loops, ch 3, 1 dc in next dc, ch 3, rep from * twice more, 3 dc in each of the next two ch-4 loops, ch 3, Sl st into 3rd ch of beg ch-6.

RND 5: With B *ch 4, 1 Sl st in the first of 6 dc group, ch 7, 1 Sl st in the last of the 6 dc group, ch 4, 1 Sl st in dc, rep from * 3 times more, ending the last Sl st into same place as first Sl st, pick up a loop with C, fasten off B.

RND 6: With C, ch 2, 4 hdc in next ch-4 sp, *5 hdc, ch 3, 5 hdc in next ch-7 sp [4 hdc in next ch-4 sp] twice, rep from * twice, 5 hdc, ch 3, 5 hdc in next ch-7 sp, 3 hdc in next ch-4 sp, join with a Sl st to 2nd ch of beg ch-2, fasten off.

JEWEL COVER

With A, ch 5, join with a Sl st to form a ring, ch 4 (counts as dc, ch 1) *1 dc, ch 1 in ring, rep from * 11 times more, fasten off leaving an 8" (20.5 cm) end for sewing. Place jewel in center of circle just made, using a tapestry needle, gather up around jewel encasing it in the yarn, attach to bottom of earring. Attach hook to top of earring.

YARN Kreinik #12 Braid, 11 yd (10 m):1 spool each, #012C (A), #012C (B), #026 (C)

HOOK Stainless steel hook #8 (1.5 mm)

GAUGE 1 square = 2" x 2" (5 x 5 cm)

NOTIONS 2 sterling silver earring hooks

2 faceted acrylic jewels

SKILL LEVEL Intermediate

BRIGHT COLORS BACKPACK

This backpack was designed and made by my granddaughter, with a little help from her mom. Nicole says it's perfect for taking all her gear to ballet lessons, and the bright colors against the denim blue background work great with jeans. The backpack is worked on a small hook so that stitches will produce a tightly woven fabric, preventing small items from slipping through.

Made with 4 colors: A, B, C, and D.

FRONT

Follow the directions for #45 Flower Garden XII Square (page 79) to make 9 squares in color combinations as follows. Always use denim mist (D) for rnd 4.

2 Foundation and Rnd 1: A, Rnd 2: C, Rnd 3: B

1 Foundation and Rnd 1: A, Rnd 2: B, Rnd 3: C

2 Foundation and Rnd 1: B, Rnd 2: A, Rnd 3: C

1 Foundation and Rnd 1: B, Rnd 2: C, Rnd 3: A

2 Foundation and Rnd 1: C, Rnd 2: B, Rnd 3: A

1 Foundation and Rnd 1: C, Rnd 2: A, Rnd 3: B

Sew squares together in 3 rows and 3 columns, using the photo as a guide.

BACK

Worked vertically.

FOUNDATION ROW: With D, ch 52, starting in 3rd ch from hook, work 1 dc in each ch across row (51 dc), turn.

ROW 1: Ch 2 (counts as dc), sk first dc, 1 dc in each of next 49 dc, 1 dc in turn ch, turn.

Rep row 1 till 13½" (34.5 cm), do not fasten off.

Holding wrong sides together, working through both thicknesses, work sc around sides and bottom of backpack, do not fasten off.

YARN	Lion Brand *Vanna's Choice Baby*, 100% acrylic, 3.5 oz (100 g)/170 yd (156 m): duckie #157 (A), 1 skein; sweat pea #169 (B), 1 skein; cheery cherry #114 (C), 1 skein; Vanna's Choice, 100% premium acrylic, 3 ozs (85 g)/145 yd (133 m): denim mist #300 (D), 2 skeins

HOOK 5/F (3.75 mm)

GAUGE 1 square = 4.5" x 4.5" (11.5 x 11.5 cm)

15 dc = 4" (10 cm)

NOTIONS 3 yd (2.8 m) of twisted nylon cord trim for straps

FINISHED SIZE 14" x 14" (35.5 x 35.5 cm)

SKILL LEVEL Easy

TOP BORDER

Ch 3 (counts as a dc, ch-1), *sk 1 st, 1 dc, ch 1 in next st, rep from * all around top edge, end with a Sl st to 2nd ch of beg ch-3, fasten off.

Cut nylon cord into two lengths and thread through ch-1 sps at top, one through front and one through back.

Thread ends together through border corners, back to front. Tie together in large knots.

Blocking not necessary.

TWEEN HOODED VEST

My granddaughter chose to use the #6 Jeannine Square for a hooded vest. She likes the textures of the square but decided to downplay the multicolor aspect a bit and use only two colors per square. By crocheting only the first three rounds of the pattern, she made squares that are smaller and more proportionate to her size. I helped her design the layout of the squares, the size adjustments, and the finishing touches.

VEST

Each square uses the first 3 rounds of Jeannine Square (page 36).

The same number of squares are made for each size; rows of dc are added at underarm to change width, rows of dc are added at bottom for length.

Rounds 2 and 3 for all squares and all finishing use MC.

Sew squares right sides together through back loops.

FOR BODY AND HOOD, MAKE:

20 squares using A for foundation and rnd 1.

16 squares using B for foundation and rnd 1.

30 squares using C for foundation and rnd 1.

HOOD

Assemble hood following the diagram, page 145.

BOTTOM HOOD BORDER

Join MC in bottom left square of hood, right side facing, work as follows:

ROW 1: Ch 3, work 1 dc in each st and in each corner sp along bottom of hood, turn.

ROW 2 (WS): Ch 4, sk 1 dc, 1 dc in next dc, *ch 1, sk 2 dc, 1 dc in next sc, rep from * around, end 1 dc in tch, turn.

YARN Plymouth *Encore DK*, 75% acrylic, 25% wool, 1.75 oz (50 g)/150 yd (138 m): #2493 (MC), 5 skeins; 1 skein each of #6002 (A), #175 (B), #1383 (C)

HOOKS 4/E (3.5 mm) for main body

9/I (5.5 mm) for tie

GAUGE 1 square = 2¾" x 2¾" (7 x 7 cm)

NOTIONS Tapestry needle

Four ⅝" (1.5 cm) buttons

Sewing needle and thread

FINISHED SIZE 10 (12, 14)

Finished chest size 28" (30", 32") (71 [76, 81.5] cm)

SKILL LEVEL Intermediate

ROW 3: Ch 3, 1 dc in each st and in each sp across row.

FOR SIZE 12: Work another row of dc.

FOR SIZE 14: Work 2 more rows of dc.

Set hood aside.

BODY

For size 12, before assembling add 1 row of dc on each side of each underarm square.

For size 14, before assembling add 2 rows of dc on each side of each underarm square.

Assemble body, following the diagram, page 145.

(continued)

BOTTOM BODY BORDER

Join MC in bottom left corner, right side facing, work bottom border as follows:

ROW 1: 1 dc in each st and in each corner sp all along bottom to Right front, turn.

For size 12 only, work 1 more row dc.

For size 14 only, work 2 more rows dc.

BEADING ROW (ALL SIZES): Ch 5, sk 2 dc, *1 dc in next st, ch 2, sk 2, rep from * across row, end 1 dc in tch, turn.

All sizes, work 1 row dc, fasten off.

Pin hood to body, centering back of hood at center back, and front of hood halfway on front squares. Sew in place.

FRONT AND HOOD BORDER

Join MC at bottom of right front. Right side facing, work 1 row sc, working 1 sc in each dc along front to top corner, work 3 sc in corner, cont sc along right top square, around hood, along left top square to corner, 3 sc in corner, cont down left front. Do not fasten off, do not turn, work 1 reverse sc all around front edge. Fasten off.

SLEEVE BORDERS

Join MC at underarm, work 1 row sc, 1 row reverse sc all around armhole, fasten off.

TIE

Using 3 strands of MC and 9/I (5.5 mm) hook, chain 150 (156, 162), fasten off. Thread tie through open row of stitches at bottom of vest.

FINISHING

Sew on buttons, using ch sps in squares as buttonholes.

If blocking is needed, lay on a padded surface, spray with water, pat into shape, allow to dry.

THE GRANNY SQUARE BOOK

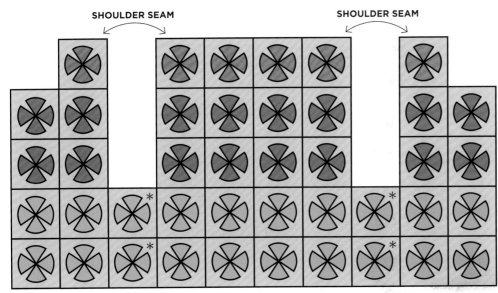

SHOULDER SEAM   SHOULDER SEAM

*ADD STITCHES TO SIDES
OF THESE SQUARES BEFORE
ASSEMBLY FOR LARGER SIZES.

Body (42 squares)

KEY

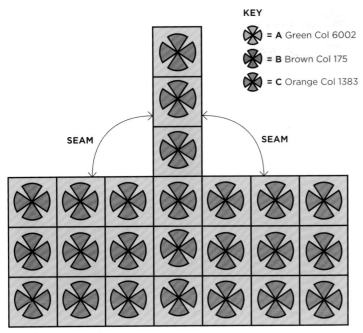

= **A** Green Col 6002

= **B** Brown Col 175

= **C** Orange Col 1383

SEAM   SEAM

Hood (24 squares)

It is easy to see why this square is called the Blooming Granny Square. The little flowers that pop up from the centers of the squares provide color and texture that are sure to please the little girl in your life.

TODDLER PULLOVER AND HAT

Made with 2 colors: A and B.

Half double crochet 2 together (hdc2tog): [Yo, insert hook in next st, yo, draw yarn through st] twice, yo, draw yarn through 5 loops on hook.

SWEATER

BACK

BOTTOM BORDER:

Make 5 #8 Blooming Granny Squares (page 38), as follows:

SQUARE 1 (MAKE 3): Work center ring and rnd 1 with A; rnd 2 with B, rnd 3 with A.

SQUARE 2 (MAKE 2): Work center ring and rnd 1 with A, rnds 2 and 3 with B.

Working through back loops of sts, sew 5 squares together in the following order to form bottom border: square 1, 2, 1, 2, and 1.

BODY:

SIZES SMALL AND LARGE ONLY:

ROW 1: With right side facing, join A in top right-hand corner of bottom border in the first corner sp, ch 2 (counts as hdc here and throughout), *[3 hdc, ch 1] in each of next 3 ch-1 sps**, 1 hdc in next corner sp, 1 hdc in seam, 1 hdc in corner sp of next square, ch 1, rep from * 3 times, rep from * to ** once, 1 hdc in last corner sp (19 groups of 3 hdc; 20 ch-1 sps), turn.

SIZE MEDIUM ONLY:

ROW 1: With right side facing, join A in top right-hand corner of bottom border in the first corner sp, ch 2 (counts as hdc here and throughout), sk next 3 dc, *[3 hdc, ch 1] in each of next 3 ch-1 sp**, 1 hdc in next corner sp, 1 hdc in seam, 1 hdc in corner sp of next square, ch 1*, rep from * once, rep from * to ** once, (3 hdc, ch 1) in each of next 2 corner sps (inc made), rep from * once, rep from * to ** once, 1 hdc in last corner sp, (20 groups of 3 hdc; 21 ch-1 sps), turn.

(continued)

YARN Lion Brand *Sock-Ease*, 75% wool, 25% nylon, 3.5 oz (100 g)/438 yd (400 m): bubblegum pink #139 (A), 2 skeins; marshmallow #100 (B), 1 skein. This amount of yarn will make both the sweater and the hat. To make the hat only, you will need only 1 skein of each color.

HOOKS F/5 (3.75 mm) for sweater sizes 2 (4)

G/6 (4 mm) for sweater size 6

E/4 (3.5 mm) for sweater collar and cuffs on all sizes

F/5 (3.75 mm) for hat

GAUGE with F/5 (3.75 mm) hook, 1 square = 2¾" x 2¾" (7 x 7 cm)

6 groups of 3 hdc and 5 ch-1 sps (23 sts) = 4" (10 cm)

With G/6 (4 mm) hook, 1 square = 3" x 3" (7.5 x 7.5 cm)

5 groups of 3 hdc and 4 ch-1 sps (19 sts) = 4" (10 cm)

NOTIONS Tapestry needle

FINISHED SIZE Sweater sizes 2 (4, 6)

Finished chest: 28" (30", 34½") (71 [76, 87.5] cm)

Hat: 16½" (42 cm) in circumference (to make larger, use a larger hook)

SKILL LEVEL
Intermediate

ALL SIZES:

ROW 2: Ch 2, 3 hdc in next ch-1 sp, ch 1, *[3 hdc, ch 1] in each ch-1 sp across to last ch-1 sp, 3 hdc in last ch-1 sp, 1 hdc in 2nd ch of turning ch, turn (20 [21, 20] groups of 3 hdc; 19 [20, 19] ch-1 sps), turn.

ROW 3: Ch 3 (counts as hdc, ch 1), [3 hdc, ch 1] in each ch-1 sp across, hdc in top of tch], turn (19 [20, 19] groups of 3 hdc; 20 [21, 20] ch-1 sps).

Rep rows 2 and 3 until back measures 10" (10½", 11") (25.5 [26.5, 28] cm) from bottom edge, ending with row 2 of patt.

ARMHOLE SHAPING:

ROW 1: Sk first st, counting each ch-1 sp as a st, Sl st over next 7 sts, ch 2, [3 hdc, ch 1] in each of next 16 (17, 16) ch-1 sp, 3 hdc in next ch-1 sp, 1 hdc next hdc, turn (17 [18, 17] groups of 3 hdc; 16 [17, 16] ch-1 sp).

Work even in pattern until armhole measures 4" (4½", 5") (10 [11.5, 12.5] cm) from beg, ending with row 2 of pattern.

LEFT NECK SHAPING:

ROW 1: Ch 3, [3 hdc, ch 1] in each of next 5 ch-1 sp, 3 hdc in next ch-1 sp, hdc in next hdc, turn.

ROW 2: Ch 2, [3 hdc, ch 1] in each of next 5 ch-1 sp, 3 hdc in next ch-1 sp, hdc in 2nd ch of tch, turn.

ROW 3: Ch 3, [3 hdc, ch 1] in each of next 4 ch-1 sp, 3 hdc in next ch-1 sp, hdc in top of tch, turn.

ROW 4: Ch 2, [3 hdc, ch 1] in each of next 4 ch-1 sp, 3 hdc in next ch-1 sp, hdc in 2nd ch of tch, turn. Fasten off.

RIGHT NECK SHAPING:

ROW 1: Sk center 7 (8, 7) ch-1 sp, sk next 2 hdc, join A in next hdc, ch 2, [3 hdc, ch 1] in each of next 6 ch-1 sp, hdc in top of tch, turn.

ROW 2: Ch 2, [3 hdc, ch 1] in each of next 5 ch-1 sp, 3 hdc in next ch-1 sp, hdc in top of tch, turn.

ROW 3: Ch 2, [3 hdc, ch 1] in each of next 5 ch-1 sp, hdc in top of tch, turn.

ROW 4: Ch 2, [3 hdc, ch 1] in each of next 5 ch-1 sp, hdc in top of tch, turn. Fasten off.

FRONT

Work same as back until armhole measures 3" (3½", 4") (7.5 [9, 10] cm), ending with row 2 of pattern.

LEFT SHOULDER SHAPING:

Work same as back left shoulder shaping. Work even in pattern across five 3-hdc groups and 4 ch-1 sp as established until armhole measures same as back armhole.

RIGHT NECK SHAPING:

Sk center 7 (8, 7) ch-1 sp, sk next 2 hdc, join A in next hdc, rep back shoulder shaping. Work even in pattern across five 3-hdc groups and 4 ch-1 sp as established until armhole measures same as back armhole.

SLEEVE (MAKE 2)

CUFF:

With E/4 (3.5 mm) hook for all sizes, make 4 small squares, working through rnd 2 only, working center ring and rnd 1 with B and rnd 2 with A. Working through back loops of sts, sew 4 squares together for cuff.

ROW 1: With right side of cuff facing, using F/5 (F/5, G/6) (3.75 [3.75, 4] mm) hook, join A in first corner sp, ch 2, 3 hdc in same sp, ch 1, *[3 hdc, ch 1] in each of next 2 ch-1 sp**, [3 hdc, ch 1] in each of next 2 corner sp, rep from * twice, rep from * to ** once, 4 hdc in last corner sp, join with a Sl st in top of beg ch-2, turn (16 hdc groups, 15 ch 1-sp).

Work even in pattern same as back until sleeve measures 9" (9½", 11") (23 [24, 28] cm) from beg. Fasten off size Large.

SIZES SMALL AND MEDIUM ONLY:

Change to G/6 (4 mm) hook and work even until sleeve measures 10" (10½") (25.5 [26.5] cm). Fasten off.

NECKBAND

Make 10 small squares same as for cuff. Working through back loops of sts, sew squares together in a strip. Then sew ends together to form a ring for collar.

FINISHING

Sew front to back at shoulders. Fold sleeves in half lengthwise, mark center top. Matching center top of sleeve to shoulder seam, pin in place, set in sleeve. Sew underarm seams. Pin collar in place, matching center square of collar to center of neck and match end seams with shoulder seams. Working through back loops of sts, sew collar into neck opening, easing in fullness.

BLOCKING: Lay sweater on a padded surface, spray lightly with water, pat into shape and allow to dry.

HAT

HAT BAND

Make 6 #8 Blooming Granny Squares (page 38) same as for bottom border of sweater, using A for center ring and rnds 1 and 3, and B for rnd 2. Working through back loops of sts, sew squares together in a strip. Then sew ends together to form a ring for hat band.

TOP OF HAT

RND 1: With right side of hat band facing, join A in any corner sp at top of hat band, ch 2, 2 hdc in same sp, ch 1, *(3 hdc , ch 1) in each of next 3 ch-1 sp**, (3 hdc, ch 1) in each of next 2 corner ch-2 sp, rep from * 4 times more, rep from * to ** once, 3 hdc in corner sp, ch 1, join with a Sl st in 2nd ch of beg ch-2.

RND 2: Ch 3, (3 hdc , ch 1) in each ch-1 sp around to last sp, 2 hdc in last ch-1 sp, join with a Sl st in the 2nd ch of beg ch-3.

RND 3: Ch 2, 2 hdc in next ch-1 sp, ch 1, (3 hdc , ch 1) in each ch-1 sp around, join with a Sl st to 3rd ch of beg ch-3.

Rep rnds 2 and 3 until crown measures 3" (7.5 cm) above hat band, ending with rnd 2 of pattern.

SHAPE CROWN:

RND 1: Ch 2, 1 hdc in next ch-1 sp, 3 hdc each ch-1 sp around, join with a Sl st in 2nd ch of beg ch-2 (90 dc).

RND 2: Ch 2, 1 hdc in each of next 7 hdc, hdc2tog over next 2 sts, *1 hdc in each of next 8 hdc, hdc2tog over next 2 sts, rep from * around, join with a Sl st in 2nd ch of beg ch-2 (81 hdc).

RNDS 3, 5, 7, AND 9: Ch 2, 1 hdc in each st around, join with a Sl st to 2nd ch of beg ch-2.

RND 4: Ch 2, 1 hdc in each of next 6 hdc, hdc2tog over next 2 sts, *1 hdc in each of next 7 hdc, hdc2tog over next 2 sts, rep from * around, join with a Sl st in 2nd ch of beg ch-2 (72 hdc).

RND 6: Ch 2, 1 hdc in each of next 5 hdc, hdc2tog over next 2 sts, *1 hdc in each of next 6 hdc, hdc2tog over next 2 sts, rep from * around, join with a Sl st in 2nd ch of beg ch-2 (63 hdc).

RND 8: Ch 2, 1 hdc in each of next 4 hdc, hdc2tog over next 2 sts, *1 hdc in each of next 5 hdc, hdc2tog over next 2 sts, rep from * around, join with a Sl st in 2nd ch of beg ch-2 (54 hdc).

RND 10: Ch 2, *hdc2tog over next 2 sts, rep from * around (27 sts). Fasten off, leaving a 12" (30.5 cm) length of yarn.

FINISHING

Thread yarn strand onto tapestry needle weave through all sts of last rnd of crown, gather together tightly, sew top together once or twice more to secure, weave in end.

This adorable baby sweater and hat set combines the technique of working a garment from the top down and using granny squares. Lighweight cotton yarn makes it comfortable for baby and easy to care for.

BABY SWEATER AND HAT

Made with 3 colors: MC, A, and B.

V-stitch (V-st): (1 dc, ch 1, 1 dc) in same st or sp.

Beginning cluster (beg cluster): Ch 3, [yo, insert hook in st or sp, yo, draw up a loop, yo, draw through 2 lps] twice in same st or sp, yo, draw through 3 loops on hook.

Cluster: [Yo, insert hook in st or sp, yo, draw up a loop, yo, draw through 2 loops on hook] 3 times in same st or sp, yo, draw through 4 loops on hook.

Single crochet 2 together (sc2tog): [Insert hook in next st, yo, draw yarn through st] twice, yo, draw yarn through 3 loops on hook.

Picot: Ch 3, sc in 3rd ch from hook.

Each V-st inc adds 2 sts. Sweater yoke is worked from the neck down.

SWEATER

Starting at neck edge, with MC, ch 58 (64).

ROW 1: 1 dc in 4th ch from hook (counts as 2 dc), 1 dc in each of next 7 (8) ch (right front section), V-st in next ch (inc made), 1 dc in each of next 9 (10) ch (right sleeve section), V-st in next ch, 1 dc in each of the next 16 (18) ch (back section), V-st in next ch, 1 dc in each of next 9 (10) ch (left sleeve section), V-st in next ch, 1 dc in each of last 9 (10) ch (left front section), turn. There will be 9 (10) dc in each front section; 9 (10) dc in each sleeve section; 16 (18) dc in back section; sections will be divided by a V-st.

ROW 2: Ch 3 (counts as a dc, now and throughout), sk first dc, *1 dc in each dc to next V-st, V-st in ch-1 sp of next V-st, rep from * 3 times, 1 dc in each dc to end, 1 dc in top of turning ch, turn.

ROWS 3-13 (3-14): Rep row 3, inc 8 sts in every row. There will be 22 (24) sts on right front, 35 (38) on sleeve, 42 (46) sts on back, 35 (38) on sleeve, 22 (24) sts on left front: 156 (170) dc plus 4 ch-1 sps total.

(continued)

YARN Tahki *Cotton Classic Lite*, 100% mercerized cotton, 1.75 oz (50 g)/146 yd (135 m): cotton candy #4443 (MC), 3 skeins; pale lemon yellow #4532 (A), 1 skein; light blue #4812 (B), 1 skein, will make both sweater and hat.

HOOKS Sweater: F/5 (3.75 mm) for size 2 and 4 yoke

F/5 (3.75 mm) for size 2 squares

G/6 (4 mm) for size 4 squares

Hat: F/5 (3.75 mm) for size 2; G/6 (4 mm) for size 4

GAUGE 1 square = 5" x 5" (12.5 x 12.5 cm) with F/5 (3.75 mm) hook

1 square = 5½" x 5½" (14 x 14 cm) with G/6 (4 mm) hook

18 dc = 4" (10 cm) with F/5 (3.75 mm) hook

NOTIONS Tapestry needle

FINISHED SIZE Sweater: sizes 2 (4)

Finished chest: 22" (24)" (56 [61] cm)

Hat: 16" (40.5 cm) in circumference; 6" (15 cm) deep for size 2

17½" (44.5 cm) in circumference, 7½" (19 cm) deep for size 4

SKILL LEVEL Intermediate

DIVIDE FOR SLEEVES AND BODY

ROW 1: Ch 3, sk first dc, dc on each of next 21 (23) sts of left front, ch 2, sk next 35 (38) dc of left sleeve, dc in each of next 42 (46) dc of back, ch 2, sk next 35 (38) dc of right sleeve, dc in each of last 21 (23) dc of right front, 1 dc in top of turning ch, turn (86 [94] dc).

ROW 2: Ch 3, sk first dc, 1 dc in each of next 21 (23) sts, 1 dc in each of next 2 ch sts at underarm, 1 dc in each of the next 42 (48) dc, 1 dc in each of next 2 ch sts at underarm, 1 dc in each of the last 21 (23) dc, 1 dc in top of turning ch, turn (90 [98] dc). Fasten off.

SQUARES

Make 4 #50 Kaleidoscope Squares (page 84) with variations as follows:

FOUNDATION: With A, ch 6, join with a Sl st to form a ring.

RND 1: With A, ch 4 (counts as dc, ch 1), [1 dc, ch 1] 7 times in ring, join with a Sl st in 3rd ch of beg ch-3 (8 ch-1 sp).

RND 2: With A, ch 3 (counts as dc), 1 dc in next ch-1 sp, *ch 2, 2 dc in next ch-1 sp, rep from * 6 times, ch 2, join with a Sl st in the 3rd ch of beg ch-3 (8 groups of 2 dc, 8 ch-1 sps). Fasten off A.

RND 3: With right side facing, join B in any ch-2 sp, ch 3, (beg cluster, ch 2, cluster, ch 2) in first sp, (cluster, ch 2, cluster, ch 2) in each ch-2 sp around, join with a Sl st in 3rd ch of beg ch-3 (8 clusters, 16 ch-2 sps). Drop B to wrong side.

RND 4: With right side facing, join MC in first ch-2 sp, ch 3, (beg cluster, ch 2, cluster) in first sp, ch 3 sk next ch-2 sp, *[1 cluster, ch 3] 3 times in next ch-2 sp**, [cluster, ch 3] twice in next ch-2 sp, sk next ch-2 sp, rep from * twice, rep from * to ** once, join with a Sl st in 3rd ch of beg ch-3 (4 groups of 3 clusters, 4 groups of 2 clusters). Drop MC to wrong side.

RND 5: With right side facing, join A in first ch-3 sp between any 2-cluster group, ch 3, 2 dc in same sp (half corner made), *ch 2, 2 dc in next ch-3 sp, (ch 1, 1 sc) in each of next 2 ch-3 sp, ch 1, 2 dc in next ch-3 sp, ch 2**, (3 dc, ch 3, 3 dc) in next ch-3 sp (corner), rep from * twice, rep from * to ** once, 3 dc in same sp as first half corner, ch 3, join with a Sl st in 3rd ch of beg ch-3. Drop A to wrong side, pick up B.

RND 6: With B, ch 1, starting in same st, *1 sc in each of next 3 dc, 2 sc in next ch-2 sp, 1 sc in each of next 2 dc, [1 sc in next ch-1 sp, 1 sc in next sc] twice, 1 sc in next ch-1 sp, 1 sc in each of next 2 dc, 2 sc in next ch-2 sp, 1 sc in each of next 3 dc, (1 sc, ch 3, 1 sc) in next ch-3 sp (corner made), rep from * around, join with a Sl st in first sc.

RND 7: With B, ch 1, 1 sc in each sc across to next corner, (1 sc, ch 3, 1 sc) in next ch-3 sp, rep from * 3 times, 1 sc in next sc, join with a Sl st in first sc (21 sc between each corner ch-3 sp). Fasten off B. Pick up MC and draw through loop on hook.

RND 8: With MC, ch 1, 1 sc in each sc across to next corner, (1 sc, ch 3, 1 sc) in next ch-3 sp, rep from * 3 times, 1 sc in each of next 2 sc, join with a Sl st in first sc (23 sc between each corner ch-3 sp). Fasten off MC.

With MC, sew 4 squares together in a strip, sew squares to bottom edge of yoke fronts and back. This will also join sleeve tops at underarms.

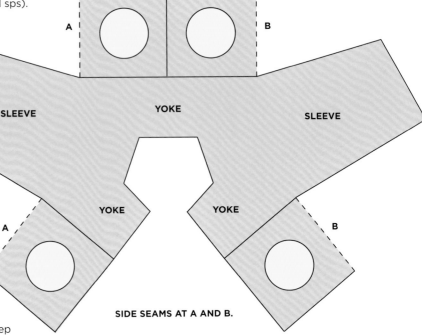

SIDE SEAMS AT A AND B.

SLEEVE (MAKE 2)

Sleeves are worked back and forth in rows, using the F/5 (3.75 mm) hook for both sizes.

With right side facing, join MC at underarm in 2nd added ch at underarm.

ROW 1: Ch 3, 1 dc in each of the next 35 (38) dc, 1 dc in the rem ch at underarm, turn 37 (40) dc.

ROW 2: Ch 3, 1 dc in each dc around, turn.

Rep row 2 until sleeve measures 5" (5½") (12.5 [14] cm) from beg. Drop MC to wrong side.

SLEEVE BORDER:

ROW 1: With right side facing, join B in first dc, ch 1, starting in same st, 1 sc in each st across, turn.

ROWS 2-8: Rep row 1 working in the following color sequence: 1 more row B, 2 rows MC, 1 row A, 1 row B, 1 row MC.

ROW 9: With MC, *ch 3, sk next sc, 1 sc in next sc, rep from * across. Fasten off, leaving a long sewing length for sewing underarm seam.

EDGING:

Edging is worked around entire outer edges of garment.

With F/5 (3.75 mm) hook for size 2, G/6 (4 mm) hook for size 4:

RND 1: With right side facing, join MC at underarm seam of bottom right side, ch 1, 1 sc in each sc along bottom of square, 3 sc in corner, 1 sc in each sc along front edge of square, sc evenly spd across row-end sts of yoke to top of right front, 3 sc in corner, sc in each st across neck edge to top of left front, 3 sc in corner, 1 sc evenly spd across row-end sts of yoke to beg of square, 1 sc in each sc along front edge of square, 3 sc in corner, 1 sc in each sc along bottom edge, join with a Sl st in first sc. Drop MC to wrong side, join B.

RND 2: With B, ch 1, sc in each sc around, working 3 sc in each corner sc, join with a Sl st in first sc.

RNDS 3-5: Rep rnd 2 working in the following color sequence: 1 rnd each of A, B, and MC.

RND 6: With MC, ch 1, sc in first sc, picot, sk next st, *1 sc in next sc, picot, sk next st, rep from * around, join with a Sl st in first sc. Fasten off.

TIE: With G/6 (hook, and all 3 colors held together as one, ch 100. Fasten off.

Weave the tie in and out of the picot row at neck, leaving ends to form a bow.

BLOCKING: Place garment on a padded surface, sprinkle lightly with water, pat into shape, using rust proof pins, pin to hold shape, allow to dry.

HAT

Make 3 Kaleidoscope Squares (page 84) in same color sequence as sweater. Join squares together to form a tube, using the Chain Join method on page (26), joining with wrong sides together so that ch is on right side of squares.

CROWN:

RND 1: With right side facing, join MC in any seam (mark this st as beg of round), ch 1, sk first st, 1 sc in each sc along top of square, 2 sc in each joining seam, join with a Sl st in first sc (80 sc).

RND 2: Ch 1, starting in same st, *1 sc in each of the next 8 sc, sc2tog over next 2 sts, rep from * around, join with a Sl st in first sc (72 sc).

RND 3: Ch 1, starting in same st, *1 sc in each of the next 8 sc, sc2tog over next 2 sts, rep from * around, join with a Sl st in first sc (64 sc).

RNDS 4-9: Continue in this manner, dec 8 sc each rnd, always having 1 st less sc between dec, until 16 sc rem. Fasten off, leaving a 12" (30.5 cm) sewing length. With tapestry needle and sewing length, weave needle though last rnd of sts, gather tight, sew top together several times to secure. Fasten off.

BOTTOM BORDER:

RND 1: With right side facing, join MC in any seam on bottom edge of hat, ch 1, 1 sc in each sc along bottom of square, 2 sc in each joining seam, join with a Sl st in first sc (81 sc).

RND 2: Ch 1, 1 sc in first sc, ch 3, (sc, ch 3) in each sc around, join with a Sl st in first sc. Fasten off.

JEANNINE SQUARE BLANKET

Blankets are the traditional use for granny squares, and I designed this one in 2005 for my book *Hooked Throws*. Far from ordinary, the Jeannine Square has some dynamic features that create lots of depth and visual texture when sewn together like this. Colors arranged in decreasing values from the square centers outward give the surface visual depth, and the double triple crochet diagonals create the illusion of a floating grid over the top of the blanket. Yarn spun from a blend of merino and alpaca fibers make this luxuriously warm and soft. Yarn companies often change their color palettes so you may not be able to match your choices with mine, but you can choose new color combination that works for you.

BLANKET

Made with 4 colors: MC, A, B, and C.

Blanket is made in 40 squares and then sewn together.

Make 40 #16 Jeannine Squares, following the directions on page 36. Using tapestry needle, sew squares tog in 8 rows of 5 squares each, sewing from WS, tbl of last row, leaving ridge on RS of work. Weave in ends.

BORDER

RND 1: With RS facing you, join MC in top right corner and, in ch-2 sp of first square, ch 1, (half corner), *work in sc tbl, working 1 sc in each st to next corner, [1 sc, ch 2, 1 sc] in corner sp, rep from * 3 times more, ending with ch 2, join with Sl st to beg ch 1, do not turn.

RND 2: Ch 3 (half corner), *work 1 dc in each st to next corner, [1 dc, ch 2, 1 dc] in corner sp, rep from * 3 times more, ending with 1 dc in next corner sp, ch 2, join with Sl st to top of beg ch 3, do not turn.

RND 3: Ch 1 (half corner), rep from * in rnd 1, fasten off.

YARN Medium-weight smooth yarn in 4 colors

Shown: Plymouth *Suri Merino*, 55% suri alpaca, 45% extrafine merino wool, 1.75 oz (50 g)/110 yd (100 m): tan #208 (MC), 6 balls; blue #5297 (A), 2 balls; orange #2037 (B), 5 balls; beige #282 (C), 4 balls

HOOK 8/H (5 mm)

GAUGE 1 square = 5" x 5" (12.7 x 12.7 cm)

NOTIONS Tapestry needle

FINISHED SIZE 30" x 46" (76 x 117 cm)

SKILL LEVEL Intermediate

PILLOWS WITH PANACHE

My daughter, like many women her age, is an expert multitasker. Besides caring for her family and their home, she is a highly skilled medical professional who still finds time for playing tennis and teaching tennis lessons. Using the Jeannine Square that I used for my blanket on page 155, she designed these two pillows, which can be crocheted in a short time but are long on décor impact. For one pillow, she simply took the basic Jeannine Square and continued the rounds to make a giant square that fits perfectly on a purchased knife-edge pillow. Her argyle pattern pillow front features nine Jeannine Squares in different color patterns turned on point. Both designs are clever and simple.

LARGE SQUARE

Follow the directions for the #6 Jeannine Square (page 36), beginning with orange yarn for foundation and rnd 1.

Use tan for rnds 3 and 4.

Omit rnd 5 and continue work as rnd 4, always having 4 more dc between corners and at the same time, working color sequence as follows:

4 rnds orange, 4 rnds brown, 4 rnds tan, 2 rnds rust, 1 rnd sc in brown.

Work 1 rnd reverse sc in brown. Fasten off.

Block square by placing on a padded surface, sprinkle with water, pat into shape.

When squares are dry, pin on pillow; sew all around outside edge just under the reverse sc, allowing the reverse sc to form welting around edge.

YARN Plymouth *Encore DK*, 75% acrylic, 25% wool, 1.75 oz (50 g), 150 yd (138 m): (for either pillow) 1 skein each of brown #6002, rust #175, orange #1383, tan #2764; to make both pillows, you will need 2 skeins of brown

HOOK 6/G (4 mm)

GAUGE 16 dc = 4" (10 cm)

NOTIONS 18" (45.5 cm) square pillows

Tapestry needle

Sewing needle and thread for sewing squares to pillow tops

FINISHED SIZE Large square = 18" x 18" (45.5 x 45.5 cm)

Each argyle square = 4½" x 4½" (11.5 x 11.5 cm)

SKILL LEVEL
Beginner

ARGYLE PILLOW

Make 9 squares as follows:

3 squares using orange for foundation and rnd 1, brown for rnd 2, orange for rnds 3 and 4, brown for rnd 5.

3 squares using rust for foundation and rnd 1, brown for rnd 2, rust for rnds 3 and 4, brown for rnd 5.

3 squares using tan for foundation and rnd 1, brown for rnd 2, tan for rnds 3 and 4, brown for rnd 5.

Block squares by placing on a padded surface, sprinkle with water, pat into shape.

When squares are dry, pin into place on pillow following photo as a guide. Sew with matching thread.

TUSCAN TILE AFGHAN

The Tuscan Tile Square used to create this unusual afghan is great for blending colors and for creating an old-world look.

Made with 3 colors: A, B, and C.

Use #58 Tuscan Tile Squares (page 93):

GROUP 1 (CENTER): Make 3 squares, foundation A, rnd 1 A, rnd 2 B, rnd 3 C, rnd 4 B, rnd 5 C.

GROUP 2 (SECOND ROUND OF SQUARES): Make 20 squares, foundation C, rnd 1 C, rnd 2 A, rnd 3 B, rnd 4 A, rnd 5 B.

GROUP 3 (OUTER GROUP OF SQUARES): Make 34 squares, foundation B, rnd 1 B, rnd 2 C, rnd 3 A, rnd 4 C, rnd 5 A.

When all squares are made, assemble afghan as follows: Sew the center 3 squares (group 1) short ends together in a strip, from the wrong side, catching back loops only.

Work border around these squares as follows:

RND 1: Join A in any corner sp, right side facing, ch 3, 1 dc in same sp (half corner), [*ch 2, 2 dc in next ch-sp, rep from * to next corner, 2 dc, ch 3, 2 dc in corner sp] 4 times, ending last repeat 2 dc, ch 3, join with a Sl st to complete corner.

RND 2: Ch 3, 1 dc in same corner sp (half corner), [*ch 2, 2 dc in next ch-2 sp, rep from * to next corner, 2 dc, ch 3, 2 dc in corner sp] 4 times, ending last rep 2 dc, ch 3, join with a Sl st to complete corner.

RNDS 3–16: Rep rnd 2, fasten off A.

Sew group 2 of squares into 4 strips of 5 squares each, pin these squares around outside edges, sew in place as before.

Work 1 rnd C, 8 rnds B around entire blanket, repeating rnds 1 through 8 of first border.

Sew group 3 of squares into 2 strips of 8 squares, 2 strips of 9 squares, pin in place around outside edges, sew in place.

Join B, work 2 rnds around entire blanket, repeating rnds 1 and 2 of first border.

BLOCKING: Lay flat on a padded surface, sprinkle with water, pat into place, using rust proof pins, pin in place, allow to dry.

YARN Naturally Caron *Country*, 75% microdenier acrylic, 25% merino wool, 3 oz (85 g)/185 yd (170 m): peacock #0021 (A), 6 skeins; berry frape #0006 (B), 5 skeins; ocean spray # 0005 (C), 3 skeins.

HOOK 5/F (3.75 mm)

GAUGE 1 square = 4¾" x 4¾" (12 x 12 cm)

6 groups of dc plus 5 ch-1 sps = 4" (10 cm)

FINISHED SIZE 45" x 60" (114.5 x 152.5 cm)

SKILL LEVEL Experienced

PLACEMATS

Move on into the dining room, and let's make some placemats. If you have solid-color dishes and you want to spice up the table a little, make your placemats with colorful yarn in the granny square border. For patterned dishes, crochet the entire placemat from one color. Cotton yarn makes them washable and lightweight.

Made with 3 colors: MC, A, and B.

SQUARES

Make 18 #21 Petite Flower Squares (page 54), using A for foundation and rnd 1, B for rnd 2, MC for rnd 3.

CENTER

FOUNDATION: With MC, chain 60, starting in 3rd ch from hook, 1 hdc in each ch, turn (58 hdc).

ROW 1: Ch 3, sk first, 1 hdc in each of next 56, 1 hdc in tch, turn.

Rep row 1 until 14" (35.6 cm) from beg.

ASSEMBLY

Sew the squares right sides together, stitching only through the back loops to form two strips of four and two strips of five. Sew four-square strips to the long sides (top and bottom) of the center panel. Then sew five-square strips to the sides.

BORDER

RND 1: Join A in any corner , work 1 rnd sc all around, making 3 sc in corner sp, end 3 sc in beg corner, join with a Sl st, pick up a loop with B, fasten off A.

RND 2: Rep rnd 1 with B, fasten off.

If blocking is needed, place on a padded surface, spray with water, pat into shape, allow to dry.

YARN Patons *Grace*, 100% cotton, 1.75 oz (50 g)/136 yd (125 m): natural #62008 (MC), 2 skeins; blush #62416 (A), 1 skein; wasabi #62244 (B), 1 skein

HOOK E/4 (3.5 mm)

GAUGE 1 square = 3½" x 3½" (9 x 9 cm)

22 hdc = 4" (10 cm)

FINISHED SIZE 21" x 17½" (53.5 x 44.5 cm)

SKILL LEVEL Easy

STAINED GLASS AFGHAN

This beautiful afghan uses a variation of the #18 Tri-Color Clusters (page 50). The combination of so many colors gives the lovely stained glass effect.

Made with 13 colors: A, B, C, D, and E. Colors C, D, and E remain the same; colors A and B are specified below for each square. Numbers correspond to numbers on chart.

All 36 squares end the same way: rnd 5 in baby fern (C); rnd 6 in black (D); rnd 7 in meadow (E); rnd 8 in black (D)

The center rounds of the squares alternate colors as follows:

1. 6 squares lilac (A), lavender frost (B)

2. 4 squares lavender frost (A), lilac (B)

3. 2 squares garnet (A), Carolina sky (B)

4. 2 squares Carolina sky (A), garnet (B)

5. 4 squares leaf green (A), rose pink (B)

6. 3 squares rose pink (A), leaf green (B)

7. 3 squares raspberry (A), leaf green (B)

8. 3 squares leaf (A), raspberry (B)

9. 3 squares violet (A), turquoise (B)

10. 3 squares turquoise (A), violet (B)

11. 1 square Carolina sky (A), baby blue (B)

12. 1 square baby blue (A), Carolina sky (B)

13. 1 square garnet (A), rose pink (B)

FOUNDATION: With A, ch 8, join with a Sl st to form a ring.

RND 1: With A, ch 3 (counts as dc) 5 dc in ring, *ch 3, 6 dc in ring, rep from * twice more, ch 3, join with a Sl st to 3rd ch of beg ch 3 (4 groups of 6 dc, 4 ch-3 sp).

RND 2: With A, ch 3 (counts as dc) [yo, insert hook into next dc, yo through 2 loops] 5 times, yo, through 6 loops, *ch 5, Sl st into 2nd ch of ch-3, ch 5, rep bet [ ] 6 times, yo thru 7 loops (cluster), rep from * twice more, end ch 5, join with a Sl st to 3rd ch of beg ch 3, (4 clusters, 8 ch-5 loops). Drop A but do not fasten off A.

RND 3: Join B to top of any cluster *work (3 dc, ch 1, 3 dc, ch 2, 3 dc, ch 1, 3 dc) into the ch-3 sp of rnd 1, Sl st in top of next cluster, rep from * 3 times more, work last Sl st in the same place as joining, pick up a loop with A, fasten off B.

(continued)

YARN Premier Yarns *Dream*, 100% Acrylic 3.5 oz (100 g)/213 yd (195 m): black #24-235 (D), 4 skeins; and 1 skein each of rose pink #24-205, raspberry #24-207, garnet #24-211, leaf green #24-214, baby fern #24-216 (C), meadow #24-217 (E), baby blue #24-221, turquoise #24-222, Carolina sky #24-223, lilac #24-226, violet #24-237, and lavender frost #24-241

HOOK 9/I (5.5 mm)

GAUGE 1 square = 7¾" x 7¾" (19.7 x 19.7 cm)

FINISHED SIZE Approximately 48" x 48" (122 x 122 cm)

SKILL LEVEL Experienced

RND 4: With A, ch 3 (counts as dc), 5 dc in the same Sl st, * (6 dc, ch 2, 6 dc) into the next ch-2 sp, 6 dc into Sl st at top of next cluster, rep from * twice more, (6 dc, ch 2, 6 dc in next ch-2 sp, join with a Sl st to 3rd ch of the beg ch 3, fasten off A.

RND 5: Join C to last Sl st of rnd 4, ch 1 (counts as 1 sc), 1 sc in each of next 5 dc, 1 sc in the ch-1 sp between the groups of dc on rnd 3, *1 sc in each of the next 6 dc, 3 sc in ch-2 sp at corner (1 sc in each of next 6 dc, 1 sc into the ch-1 sp between groups of dc on rnd 3) twice, rep from * twice more, 1 sc in ea of next 6 dc, 3 sc in ch-2 sp at corner, 1 sc in ea of the next 6

dc, 1 sc in ch-1 sp between groups of dc on rnd 3, join with a Sl st to first ch, pick up a loop with D, fasten off C.

RND 6: With D, ch 1 (counts as a sc), work 1 sc in each of next 14 sc, *1 sc, ch 2, 1 sc in next st (corner), 1 sc in each of next 22 sc, rep from * twice more, 1 sc, ch 2, 1 sc in next st (corner), 1 sc in each of next 7 sc, join with a Sl st to beg ch 1, end D, pick up a loop with E, do not fasten off D.

RND 7: With E, ch 1 (counts as a sc), work 1 sc in each of next 15 sc, *1 sc, ch 2, 1 sc in next st (corner), 1 sc in each of next 24 sc, rep from * twice more, 1 sc, ch 2, 1 sc in next st (corner), 1 sc in each of next 8 sc, join with a Sl st to beg ch 1, pick up a loop with D, fasten off E.

RND 8: With D, ch 1 (counts as a sc), work 1 sc in each of next 16 sc, *1 sc, ch 2, 1 sc in next st (corner), 1 sc in each of next 26 sc, rep from * twice more, 1 sc, ch 2, 1 sc in next st (corner), 1 sc in each of next 9 sc, join with a Sl st to beg ch 1, fasten off.

When all squares are made, follow chart for color placement.

Join squares holding wrong sides together, and working from the right side, work in sc through both loops of last sc row on squares, continue till you have 6 squares joined, repeat until you have 6 rows of 6 squares. Work in the same manner to join strips crosswise.

BORDER:
Join black yarn in any corner sp and ch 1 (counts as sc) *sk 2 sc, 7 dc in next sc, sk 2 sc, 1 sc in next sc, rep from * all around, join with a Sl st to beg ch-1, fasten off.

BLOCKING:
Lay afghan on a padded surface and spray with water, pat into shape using your hands, using rustproof pins, pin down, allow to dry.

FLOWER GARDEN THROW

Flowers have been my inspiration for many years, and I use the theme a lot. Nothing cheers up a room more than flowers, and this flower garden throw will brighten any corner. I have included twelve flower garden squares in this book—#34 through #45—though only six of them were used for this throw. For this design, same-flower squares are arranged in diagonal rows. You might choose to design yours with some of the other flower garden squares.

FLOWER GARDEN SQUARES

Make 6 each of the following Flower Garden Squares:

#34 Flower Garden Square I (page 69), using A for foundation, rnds 1 and 2, C for rnds 3-5, B for rnds 5-7, A for rnd 8.

#37 Flower Garden Square IV (page 70), using H for foundation and rnds 1-3, C for rnds 4-6, B for rnds 7 and 8, A for rnd 9. When square is completed, tack down a few petals from behind.

#38 Flower Garden Square V (page 71), using F for foundation and rnds 1 and 2. C for rnds 3, 4 and 5, B for rnds 6 and 7, A for rnd 8.

#39 Flower Garden Square VI (page 72), using A for foundation and rnds 1-3, D for rnd 4, C for rnds 5-7, B for rnds 8 and 9, A for rnd 10.

#41 Flower Garden Square VIII (page 75), using C for foundation and rnd 1, G for rnd 2, E for rnds 3 and 4, C for rnds 5-7, B for rnds 8 and 9, A for rnd 10. When square is completed, tack down a few petals from behind.

#44 Flower Garden Square XI (page 78), using C for foundation and rnd 1, G for rnds 2 and 3, C for rnds 4 and 5, B for rnds 6 and 7, A for rnd 8.

Assemble squares following the diagram using the Chain Join method shown on page 26.

(continued)

YARN Red Heart *Soft Yarn*, 100% acryllic, 5 oz (140 g)/256 yd (234 m): lavender #3720 (A), 3 skeins; dark leaf #9523 (B), 2 skeins; leaf #9522 (C), 2 skeins; and lilac #9528 (D), turquoise #2515 (E), pink #6768 (F), honey #9114 (G), and tangerine #4422 (H), 1 skein each

HOOK 8/H (5 mm)

GAUGE 1 square = 6" x 6" (15 x 15 cm)

FINISHED SIZE Approximately 44" x 44" (112 x 112 cm)

SKILL LEVEL Intermediate

To complement the frilly, flowery theme of this throw, I've added a scallop border with picot edging. Follow my color scheme or create a flower garden in your favorite hues.

BORDER

RND 1: With A, join with a Sl st in any corner sp, ch 3, 1 dc in same sp (half corner made) [*sk 2 sc, 1 dc in next sc, ch 2, rep from * to next corner sp, 2 dc, ch 3, 2 dc in corner], rep bet [ ] on rem 3 sides, end last rep 2 dc, ch 3 in first half corner sp, join with a Sl st to complete corner.

RND 2: Ch 3, work 2 dc in space to right of ch-3 (half corner) *[ch 2, sk 2, 1 dc in next dc] 52 times, ch 2, 3 dc, ch 3, 3 dc in corner sp, rep from * 3 times more ending last rep 3 dc in same sp as beg half corner, ch 3, join with a Sl st to 3rd ch of beg ch 3 to complete corner, fasten off A.

RND 3: Join C with a Sl st in any corner sp, *ch 5, sk 2 dc, 1 sc in next dc [ch 5, sk next dc, 1 dc in next dc] 27 times, ch 5, 1 sc in corner sp (29 ch-5 sps), rep from * 3 times more, end last rep Sl st in the beg Sl st.

RND 4: With C, work 7 sc in each ch-5 sp around, end with a Sl st to first sc, fasten off C.

RND 5: Join A with a Sl st in any corner sc, working from the back loop, sk 1 sc, *1 sc in each of next 3 sc, ch 3, 1 sc in same sc as ch 3 (picot made), 1 sc in ea of next 2 sc, sk 2 sc, rep from * all around, join with a Sl st to beg Sl st, fasten off.

Blocking is not recommended for this throw.

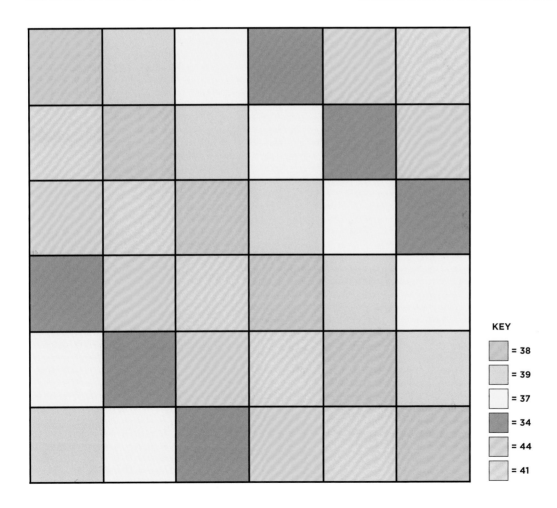

KEY

	= 38
	= 39
	= 37
	= 34
	= 44
	= 41

LILY POND AFGHAN

When I first saw this little square it reminded me of lily pads floating in a pond. I loved the picture my mind formed, so I designed this afghan.

Made with 3 colors used 2 at a time: A and B.

Triple crochet 2 together (tr2tog): (Yo hook twice, pick up a loop in next stitch yo thru 2 loops, yo through 2 loops) twice, yo, through all 3 loops on hook.

LILY POND FOUR-SQUARE SETS

Using English garden as A and sprout as B, make 52 #12 Lily Pond Squares (page 43). Use A for foundation, rnds 1 and 2; use B for rnds 3 and 4. Sew four squares together to create larger square. Make 13 four-square sets in this manner. For each set, continue as follows:

RND 1: Join B in any corner sp, ch 3, make 2 dc same sp (half corner), [ch 2, 1 dc bet 8 sts of petal, ch 2, 1 tr in dip, ch 2, 1 dc bet petals, ch 2, 1 dc next ch-sp of petal, ch 2, 1 dc next ch-sp of petal, ch 2, 1 dc in center, ch 2, 1 tr in dip, ch 2, 1 dc, bet petals, ch 2], 3 dc, ch 3, 3 dc in next ch-5 sp (corner) rep from * twice more, rep bet [ ] once, 3 dc, ch 2, in same sp as beg half corner, ch 2, join Sl st to 3rd ch of beg ch-3 to complete corner.

RND 2: Ch 3, make 2 dc slightly back in sp, * ch 2, [2 dc, ch 1, next ch-2 sp] 8 times, 2 dc next sp, ch 2, 3 dc, ch 3, 3 dc, rep from * twice more, ch 2, rep bet [ ] once, 2 dc next ch-2 sp, ch 2, 3 dc, ch 3, in same sp as first corner, ch 3, join Sl st to top of ch 3 to complete corner, fasten off.

CIRCLE SQUARES

Make 12 using coral as A, sprout as B

FOUNDATION: With A, ch 4, join with a Sl st to form a ring.

RND 1: With A, working in ring, ch 4, 1 tr (counts as first petal), ch 3, *1 tr2tog, ch 3, rep from * 6 times more, join with a Sl st to 3rd ch of beg ch 4 (8 petals), fasten off A.

RND 2: With B, join in any ch-3 sp, 1 sc same sp *ch 5, 1 sc in next ch-3 sp, rep from * 6 times more, ch 5, join with a Sl st to beg ch 1, (eight ch-5 sp).

(continued)

YARN Lion Brand *Baby Wool*, 100% total easy care wool, 1.75 oz (50 g)/98 yd (90 m): sprout #174, 17 skeins; coral #103, 3 skeins; English garden #203, 8 skeins (note that the prints colors have only 1.4 oz [40 g]/79 yd [72 m])

HOOK 8/H (5 mm)

GAUGE Square = 9" x 9" (23 x 23 cm)

FINISHED SIZE 47" x 47" (119.5 x 119.5 cm) including border.

SKILL LEVEL: Intermediate

RND 3: With B, Sl st in first 3 ch of next ch-5, ch 4 (counts as dc, ch 1), * [tr2 tog, ch 1, 5 times in next ch-5 sp, ch 1], 1 dc in next ch-5 sp, ch 1, rep from * 2 times more, then rep bet [ ] once, join with a Sl st to 3rd ch of beg ch 4.

RND 4: With B, ch 3 (counts as 1 tr) 1 tr in same st, (half corner made) ch 1, * [1 dc in next sp between petals, ch 1] 4 times, * 2 tr, ch 2, 2 tr in next tr, (corner made) ch 1, rep from * twice more, rep between [ ], end 2 tr in same st as beg ch 3, ch 2, join with a Sl st to 3rd ch of beg ch 3 (completes first corner).

RND 5: With B, ch 3, 2 dc slightly back to corner *[ch 1, 2 dc in next sp] 5 times, ch 1, 3 dc, ch 2, 3 dc in corner, rep from * twice, rep bet [ ], end 3 dc, ch 2, join with a Sl st to 3rd ch of beg ch 3.

RNDS 6 AND 7: With B, rep rnd 5. With each rnd, there will be an additional repeat on each side of square.

RND 8: With A, rep rnd 7. There will be an additional repeat on each side of square.

RND 9: With B, rep rnd 8. There will be an additional repeat on each side of square. Fasten off.

Sew all squares together with right sides together, sewing through one loop only to form ridge on right side.

BORDER

RND 1: With sprout, join yarn in any corner, ch 3, 2 more dc in same sp (half corner made), ch 1 *[2 dc in next ch-1 sp, ch 1] 10 times, [2 dc in next corner ch-3 sp, ch 1] twice, rep from * 3 times more [2 dc in next ch-1 sp, ch 1] 10 times, 3 dc, ch 3, 3 dc in next ch-3 sp (full corner made), rep from * 3 times more, ending last rep 3 dc, ch 3, join in the 3rd ch of beg ch-3 to complete corner, do not fasten off, pick up a loop with coral.

RND 2: With coral 1 sc in ea dc, 1 sc in ea ch-1 sp, 2 sc, ch 3, 2 sc in each corner sp around, pick up a loop with sprout, fasten off coral.

RND 3: With sprout 1 sc in each sc around, 2 sc, ch 3, 2 sc in each corner sp, fasten off.

Do not press. If blocking is needed, lay on a padded surface, sprinkle with water and gently pat into shape, allow to dry.

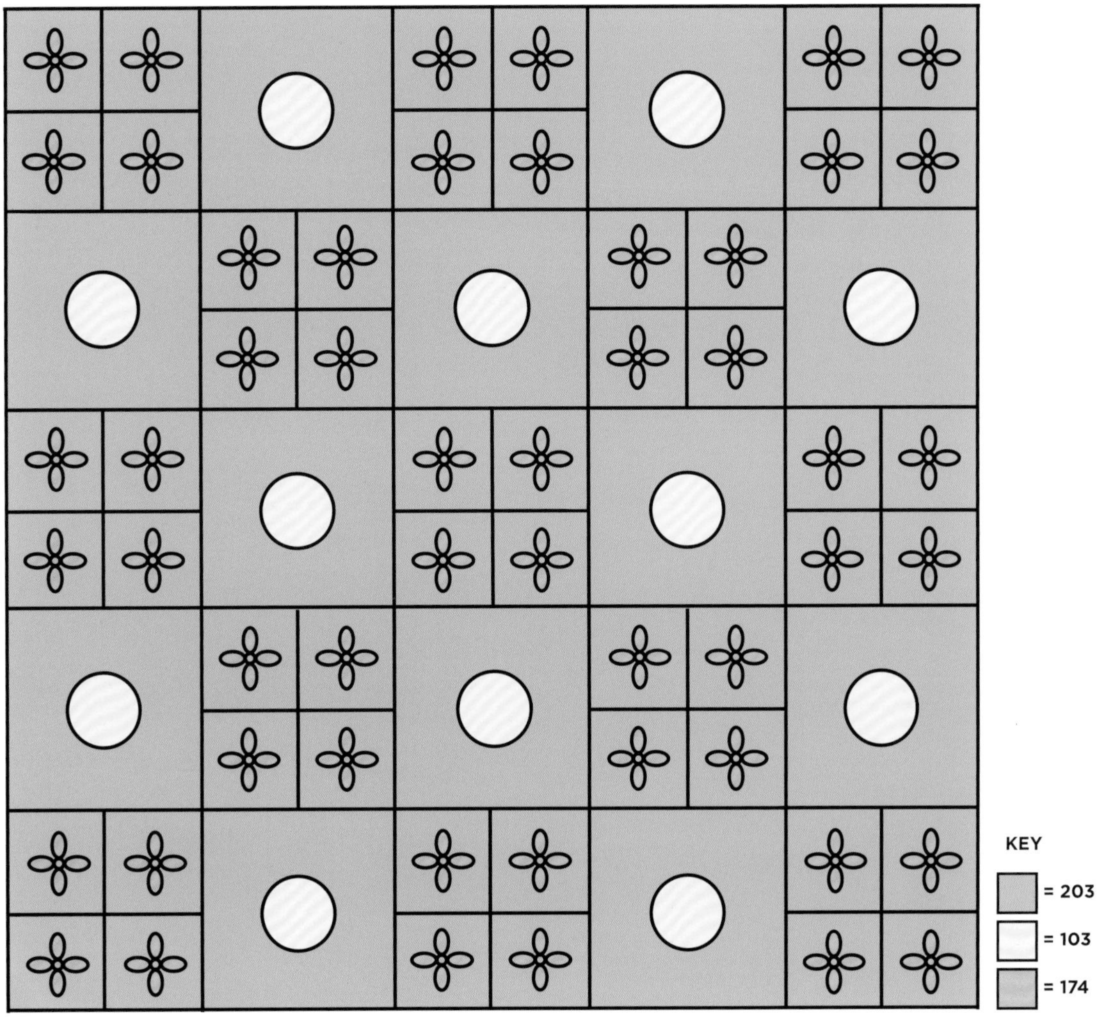

KEY

= 203

= 103

= 174

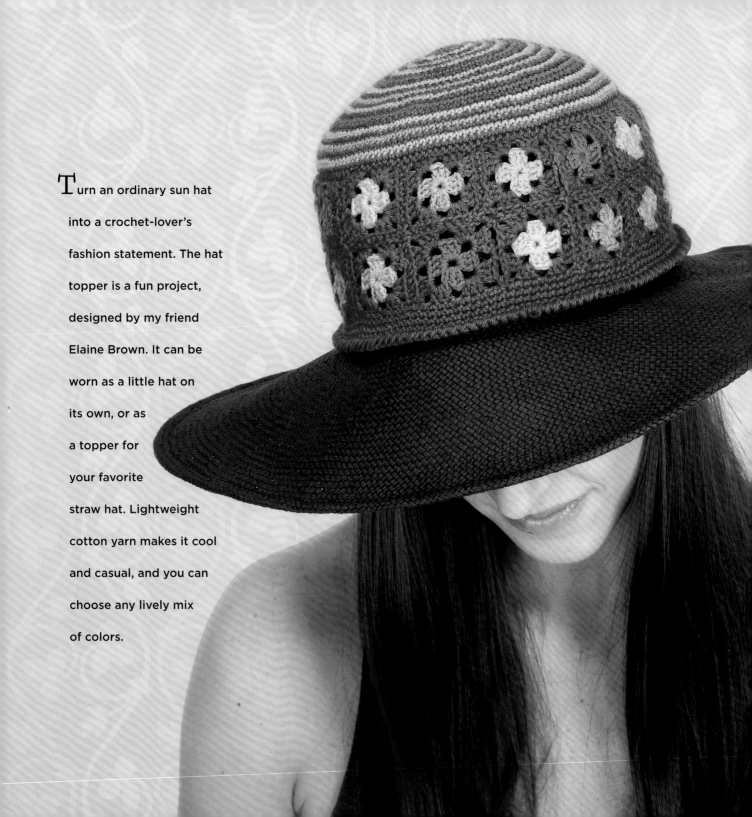

Turn an ordinary sun hat into a crochet-lover's fashion statement. The hat topper is a fun project, designed by my friend Elaine Brown. It can be worn as a little hat on its own, or as a topper for your favorite straw hat. Lightweight cotton yarn makes it cool and casual, and you can choose any lively mix of colors.

STRAW HAT TOPPER

DESIGNED BY ELAINE BROWN

Made with 5 colors: MC, A, B, C, and D.

Reverse single crochet (rev sc): Working from left to right, insert hook in next st to the right, yo, draw yarn through st, yo, draw yarn through 2 loops on hook.

GRANNY SQUARE BAND

Make 7 of each using A, B, C, and D for CC (28 squares total)

With CC, ch 4, join with Sl st to form ring.

RND 1: Ch 3 (counts as dc), work 2 dc in ring, ch 3, (3 dc, ch 3) 3 times in ring, join with a Sl st in 3rd ch of beg ch-3. Fasten off.

RND 2: With right side facing, join MC in any ch-3 corner sp, ch 3, (2 dc, ch 3, 3 dc) in ch-3 sp, ch 1 (3 dc, ch 3, 3 dc, ch 1) in each ch-3 sp around, join with a Sl st in 3rd ch of beg ch-3. Fasten off.

With right sides facing, using MC, working through back loops only, whip st squares together following assembly diagram. This leaves the front loops free on the right side to accent each square. Then sew the first squares to the last squares to form a ring.

CROCHET HAT COVER—CENTER

GAUGE Rounds 1 7 = 2" (5 cm) in diameter

Work in the following color sequence: 1 rnd each of *MC, A, MC, B, MC, C, MC, D, rep from * throughout.

With MC, ch 2.

RND 1 (RIGHT SIDE): 6 sc in 2nd ch from hook, join with a Sl st in first sc (6 sc). Do not fasten off MC. Carry MC up on wrong side of work.

(continued)

YARN Patons *Grace*, 100% cotton, 1.75 oz (50 g)/136 yd (125 m), 1 skein of each: orchid #62307 (MC); azure #62104 (A); ginger #62027 (B); viola #62322 (C); lemon lime #62222 (D).

HOOK C/2 (2.75 mm)

GAUGE 1 square = 1½" x 1½" (4 x 4 cm)

NOTIONS Tapestry needle

FINISHED SIZE 23" (58.5 cm) in circumference.

SKILL LEVEL Intermediate

KEY

 = A

 = B

 = C

= D

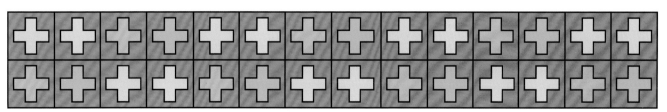

RND 2: With right side facing, join A in first sc, ch 1, 2 sc in each sc around, join with a Sl st in first sc (12 sc). Fasten off.

RND 3: With MC, ch 1,*sc in sc, 2 sc in next sc, rep from * around, join with a Sl st in first sc (18 sc).

RND 4: With right side facing, join B in first sc, ch 1, *sc in next 2 sc, 2 sc in next sc, rep from * around, join with a Sl st in first sc (24 sc). Fasten off.

RND 5: With MC, ch 1, sc in next sc, *2 sc in next sc, sc in next 3 sc, rep from * around, ending with sc in last 2 stc, join with a Sl st in first sc (30 sc).

RND 6: With right side facing, join C in first sc, ch 1, *2 sc in next sc, sc in next 4 sc, rep from * around, join with a Sl st in first sc (36 sc). Fasten off.

RND 7: With MC, ch 1, *sc in next 5 sc, 2 sc in next sc, rep from * around, join with a Sl st in first sc (42 sc).

RND 8: With right side facing, join D in first sc, ch 1, sc in next 3 sc, *2 sc in next sc, sc in next 6 sc, rep from * around, ending with sc in each of last 3 sc, join with a Sl st in first sc (48 sc). Fasten off.

RNDS 9–23: Maintaining color sequence, work in sc, inc 6 sc in each rnd as established, stagger the position of the increases so as not to work inc over inc in the previous rnd (138 sc at end of last rnd).

RND 24: With right side facing, join D in first sc, ch 1, sc in each sc around, join with a Sl st in first sc. Fasten off.

RND 25: With MC, ch 1, sc in each sc around, join with a Sl st in first sc. Fasten off.

With right sides of the hat center and the granny square band facing, join the two pieces together by working a round of Sl sts through inside loops of each side together, join with a Sl st in first Sl st. Fasten off.

BOTTOM TRIM

With right side facing, join MC with a Sl st to the bottom back of the granny square band.

RNDS 1–3: Ch 1, sc in each st and sp around, join with a Sl st in first sc (126 sc).

RND 4: Working from left to right, ch 1, reverse sc in each st around, join with a Sl st in first reverse sc. Fasten off.

INDEX